The Case for Withdrawal From Afghanistan

Edited by Nick Turse

VERSO

London • New York

First published by Verso 2010
© the collection Verso 2010
© individual contributions the contributors

The moral rights of the authors have been asserted

1 3 5 7 9 10 8 6 4 2

Verso
UK: 6 Meard Street, London W1F 0EG
US: 20 Jay Street, Suite 1010, Brooklyn, NY 11201
www.versobooks.com

Verso is the imprint of New Left Books

ISBN-13: 978-1-84467-451-0

British Library Cataloguing in Publication Data
A catalogue record for this book is available from the British Library

Library of Congress Cataloging-in-Publication Data
A catalog record for this book is available from the Library of Congress

Typeset in Minion Pro by Hewer Text UK Ltd, Edinburgh
Printed in the US by Maple Vail

The Case for Withdrawal
From Afghanistan

CONTENTS

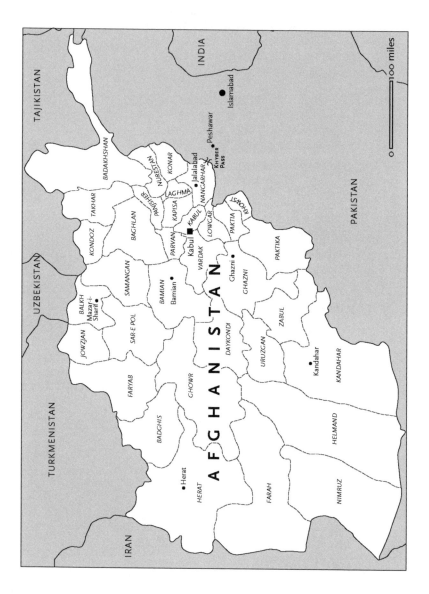

TAJIKISTAN

INDIA

Islamabad

Peshawar

KHYBER
PASS

BADAKHSHAN

NURESTAN

KONAR

Jalalabad

NANGARHAR

PANJSHER

LAGHMAN

KAPISA

TAKHAR

KONDOZ

BAGHLAN

PARVAN

KHOST

KABUL

Kabul

LOWGAR

PAKTIA

UZBEKISTAN

SAMANGAN

BAMIAN

Bamian

VARDAK

Ghazni

GHAZNI

PAKTIKA

BALKH

Mazar-i-
Sharif

SAR-E POL

DAYKONDI

PAKISTAN

JOWZJAN

ZABUL

FARYAB

URUZGAN

GHOWR

Kandahar

KANDAHAR

BADGHIS

A F G H A N I S T A N

HELMAND

TURKMENISTAN

Herat

HERAT

FARAH

NIMRUZ

IRAN

100 miles

0

INTRODUCTION

In February 2010, as this book was being prepared, nearly 15,000 US, British, Canadian, and allied Afghan troops were in the midst of a much-publicized offensive against several hundred Taliban fighters in the town of Marjah in Helmand Province in Southern Afghanistan.[1] More than eight years had passed since President George W. Bush first put US boots on the ground in that long-ravaged country, and since taking office in January 2009, President Barack Obama had repeatedly escalated the conflict, increasing troop numbers, boosting air strikes by unmanned drones, and sending more CIA agents and covert operators into the country. As he did so, opposition to the war in allied NATO countries continued to rise, as Canada—the third largest foreign force in Afghanistan—declared it would withdraw its 2,800 soldiers by the end of 2011 and the Dutch government collapsed under the weight of anti-war sentiment.[2] After ordering a troop surge of 30,000 in late 2009—against the counsel of retired Lieutenant General Karl W. Eikenberry, his ambassador to Afghanistan who had previously served as the top American military commander there—he had indisputably turned Bush's war into his own, for which Marjah was to be the first major operation of his new "surge."[3]

1   Atia Abawi, "NATO Launches Major Offensive in Afghanistan," CNN. com, February 12, 2010, and Miguel Marquez, et al., "Marines Attack Taliban-Held City," ABCNews.go.com, February 12, 2010.
2   Theunis Bates, "As Dutch Quit Afghanistan, Will Other Allies Follow?" AOLNews.com, February 22, 2010.
3   Eric Schmitt, "U.S. Envoy's Cables Show Worries on Afghan Plans," *New York Times*, January 25, 2010.

In the weeks before the Marjah Offensive, the Americans had purposely tele-graphed their plan to take the populated enclave by force and then "roll in" with, according to General Stanley McChrystal, the then commander of the US-led International Security Assistance Force (ISAF), "a government in a box."[4] It was to be a marquee operation in McChrystal's counterinsurgency (COIN) strategy to clear militants from population centers and bring in security, economic devel-opment, and government services to win Afghan hearts and minds.

Five days into the fight—the largest joint operation by US, coalition, and Afghan troops since the Taliban were driven from power in 2001—the Marines and their indigenous allies were being slowed up by a group of committed Taliban snipers who were merely delaying what was seen as inevitable: a US victory that would allow the prefabricated government to take power.[5] While the Marines fought, and a few died, to take the town of 50,000—using mortars, artillery, helicopter gunships, unmanned drones, and fixed-wing aircraft against enemies armed with little more than rifles and homemade bombs—the town's mayor-in-waiting, Abdul Zahir Aryan, also known as Haji Zahir (who spent fifteen years in Germany, four of them in a prison for stabbing a family member) was living at a US military base elsewhere in Helmand waiting for the day he and a team of four American "mentors" assigned to assist him would take control of the city.[6]

---

4   Ben Arnoldy, "Marjah Offensive: Q&A on Why It Matters to Afghanistan War," *Christian Science Monitor*, February 9, 2010; and Andrew J. Bacevich, " 'Government in a box' in Marja," *Los Angeles Times*, February 17, 2010.

5   C. J. Chivers, "Snipers Imperil U.S.-Led Forces in Afghan Offensive," *New York Times*, February 17, 2010.

6   C. J. Chivers, "Afghans Voice Their Fears Amid Marja Campaign," *New York Times*, February 21, 2010; Chivers, "Snipers Imperil U.S.-Led Forces in Afghan Offensive"; Christopher Drew, "Drones Are Playing a Growing Role in Afghanistan," *New York Times*, February 19, 2010; Rajiv Chandrasekaran, "Taliban Resistance Slows Coalition Forces in Marja, Afghanistan," *Washington Post*, February 18, 2010; Matthew Rosenberg and Michael Phillips, "Coalition Prepares to Set Up Authority in Marjah," *Wall Street Journal*, February 18, 2010; Joshua Partlow and Jabeen Bhatti, "New top official in Marja, Afghanistan, was convicted of stabbing stepson," *Washington Post*, March 6, 2010; "Afghan: Marjah Chief's Crime Record Will Be Probed," Associated Press, March 6, 2010.

This wasn't the first time that foreigners had looked to leave their mark on Marjah. It wasn't even the first time that American "mentors" had come to the region to remake it as they saw fit. A March 1960 *New York Times* article noted that US technical aid was being supplied to agricultural projects in the Marjah area, part of a Cold War campaign against the Soviet Union to win Afghan hearts and minds by building everything from dams and canals to American-style suburban subdivisions. That year, the celebrated British historian Arnold Toynbee visited Helmand and pronounced the projects there to be "a piece of America inserted into the Afghan landscape." He continued, "The new world that they are conjuring up at the Helmand River's expense is to be an America-in-Asia."[7]

Marjah was actually a rare bright spot in that Cold War aid competition—at least for a time. All around it, joint US–Afghan efforts—$100,000,000 worth—had faltered badly. Post–World War II plans to turn "a rocky desert into fertile fields of wheat, cotton, corn and rice" had been dogged by numerous setbacks that resulted in "frustration and a tinge of despair." The problem, according to the *Times* report, was that the "human element was largely overlooked." Nomads were to be turned into farmers, but "many tribesmen were found to like their itinerant lives of freedom." On top of that, agricultural training efforts were at best spotty, American advice was flawed, US infrastructure failed and the foreign efforts were poorly coordinated with locals.[8] A 1988 study of American assistance to Afghanistan from 1950–1979, funded by the US Agency for International Development (USAID), would conclude that shortages of qualified personnel and unrealistic expectations undermined efforts, while major investments in strengthening the country's public administration failed. The report found that:

The US generally had too much confidence in the applicability of technical solutions to complex social and economic development problems and of the

7   Adam Curtis, "Kabul: City Number One—Part 3," BBC.co.uk, October 13, 2009; David Rohde and Carlotta Gall, "Afghan Symbol for Change Becomes a Symbol of Failure," *New York Times*, September 5, 2006; and "Mistakes Beset Afghan Project," *New York Times*, March 13, 1960.
8   "Mistakes Beset Afghan Project"; and Curtis, "Kabul: City Number One—Part 3."

appropriateness and transferability of US values and experience. This over-confidence . . . meant that too little attention was paid to local circumstances and values in the preparation and execution of aid activities.[9]

The American efforts in Helmand continued into the 1970s as the US attempted to sway the Afghans away from ties with the Soviet Union which, fearing US designs on Afghanistan, focused ever more attention on a nation that bordered its vulnerable Central Asian republics. Afghan leaders, for their part, were only too happy to play the two superpowers against one another to advance their own interests. As a result, Afghanistan became one of the largest per capita recipients of foreign aid on the planet.[10]

Just over twenty years after that *New York Times* article mentioning Marjah was published, word of the efforts of another contingent of foreigners in the region made its way into the Near East/North Africa Report No. 2361 from the US Central Intelligence Agency's Foreign Broadcast Information Service. A June 8, 1981 *Pakistan Times* article, reprinted in the government report, recounted military operations in Helmand Province by Afghan "Mujahideen"—"soldiers of God," or, in American parlance, "Freedom Fighters"—against the Soviet military forces that had invaded the country in late 1979. A "night raid" on a Soviet camp had destroyed three tanks and netted the Afghan guerrillas two Soviet Kalashnikov rifles as well as ammunition. The article continued:

> In Marjah area of the province, the Mujahideen are fighting against Soviets who are using artillery as well.
>
> In an encounter taking place on May 25, the Soviet casualties were five while one Mujahid was martyred.[11]

---

9 Quoted in Andrew Wilder, ed., "Losing Hearts and Minds in Afghanistan," in *Middle East Institute Viewpoints: Afghanistan, 1979–2009: In the Grip of Conflict*, Washington, DC: The Middle East Institute, 2009, 143.
10 Rohde and Gall, "Afghan Symbol for Change Becomes a Symbol of Failure"; "Mistakes Beset Afghan Project"; and Curtis, "Kabul: City Number One—Part 3"; Wilder, "Losing Hearts and Minds in Afghanistan," 144.
11 Foreign Broadcast Information Service, Near East/North Africa Report No. 2361, July 9, 1981.

The next year, a news release by the pro-mujahideen, London-based Afghan News Agency stated that Afghan guerrillas had recently killed a seemingly unbelievable 600 Soviet and allied Afghan troops during a three-day battle in Helmand Province and, in retaliation, Soviet forces had set fire to homes and killed 200 civilians in Marjah.[12]

After almost a decade of bloody conflict, the Soviet military finally withdrew from Afghanistan in 1989. The continuing civil war afterward eventually saw the rise of the Islamic fundamentalist Taliban—a name derived from a Persian word meaning Islamic students or seekers—and their seizure of the Afghan capital, Kabul, in 1996.[13] Following the attacks of September 11, 2001, planned by al Qaeda militants in Afghanistan (as well as Germany and the United States), the US launched strikes, coordinated with Afghan opposition forces, that chased the Taliban from power, before sending in a sizeable contingent of ground forces to garrison the country.

Twenty years after the report of a Soviet massacre, Marjah was again in the news and troops armed with Kalashnikovs were back in town. This time, they were Afghan security forces dispatched by a weak central government to impose the will of foreign interests. Without the Taliban—who had banned poppy cultivation two years before—in control, those fields around Marjah in which Americans long ago had promised to help grow wheat, cotton, corn, and rice, were now filled with opium poppies, helping the country rise to become the world's number one narco-state.

Under pressure from the United Nations, the US, and its allied coalition partners, Afghan troops "[a]rmed with assault rifles and fistfuls of American dollars" rolled into Marjah. For the poor farmers there—most of them from the Pashtun ethnic group—poppies were their lone salvation, but the troops had come to see the poppy fields destroyed and offered hopelessly small sums in compensation. "They have gunmen, they have cars, they have force," a young farmer told the Associated Press. "We have no option."[14]

---

12   "600 Reported Killed in Afghan," *Sarasota Herald-Tribune*, May 26, 1982.
13   Milton Bearden, "Afghanistan, Graveyard of Empires," *Foreign Affairs*, November 2001/December 2001.
14   Christopher Torchia, "Under Armed Guard, Afghan Poppy Eradication Program Gets Under Way," Associated Press, April 10, 2002.

Despite the eradication campaign, Marjah quickly became a major center of poppy cultivation again. In response, and echoing the grand dreams of those joint US–Afghan ventures of the mid-twentieth century, in 2007 the US-allied Afghan government announced twenty-three rural development projects in and around Marjah—including the cleaning of canals, the upkeep of mosques, and improving the water supply.[15] By 2010, however, the promised fruits of these various schemes, just like the earlier American dream of amber waves of grain, had yet to take hold as Americans fought their way back into town.

Not surprisingly, it also looked like the "human element" was again being "largely overlooked." Local Afghans, for instance, told an Associated Press reporter that they weren't interested in being liberated from Taliban control. "The Taliban didn't create any problems for people," said Samad Khan, a fifty-five-year-old poppy farmer living on the outskirts of Marjah. Townspeople, instead, worried about the fighting and the potential for devastation. Mohammad Salam, a former provincial council member in Helmand Province and Marjah resident, told the AP, "The poor people from Marjah are caught between two big pressures: the Taliban and the Afghan government and international forces. This is not good for people."[16]

The battle for Marjah was envisioned as a template for future operations. In Taliban-controlled towns all across southern Afghanistan, US, NATO, and Afghan troops loyal to the government of Afghan President Hamid Karzai planned on setting up government-in-a-box franchises and, after almost a decade of largely futile fighting, embarking on the road to true and lasting victory. As recent history indicates, however, foreign plans for Marjah never quite seem to go as expected, just as foreign designs on Afghanistan, from those of Alexander the Great and Genghis Khan to the British and the Soviet Union, more generally have gone off track, normally with much blood spilled.[17]

---

15   "Afghan Official Says Hundreds of Projects Under Way in Helmand," from the text of report by Afghan state-run newspaper *Anis* on June 21, 2007, BBC Monitoring South Asia, June 23, 2007.

16   Alfred de Montesquiou and Rahim Faiez, "Taliban town residents skeptical of NATO promises," Associated Press, February 17, 2010.

17   Bearden, "Afghanistan, Graveyard of Empires."

Today, a counterinsurgency or COIN strategy, based on the US military delivering nation–building-style development and aid, has been embraced by McChrystal's successor General David Petraeus and his commander-in-chief President Obama. As it happens, though, current American COIN operations have a painfully familiar ring, bringing to mind past failed hearts and minds strategies. That 1988 USAID-funded report on American assistance to Afghanistan from 1950–1979, for example, concluded:

> The use of aid for short-term political objectives, in the competition with the Soviet Union in Afghanistan, tended to distort sound economic rationale for development, and in the process to weaken the longer-term political interests of the United States.[18]

As Andrew Wilder, a Pakistani-born expert on Afghanistan and Research Director at the Feinstein International Center at Tufts University, notes: "Given the centrality to the counterinsurgency (COIN) strategy of the assumption that aid is an important stabilization tool, and the billions of development dollars allocated based on this assumption, there is surprisingly limited evidence from Afghanistan that supports it." He continues:

> To begin with, there is little evidence that poverty or a lack of reconstruction are major causes of the insurgency in Afghanistan, so it is not at all clear how reconstruction projects can be effective in addressing the insurgency . . . the assumption is also not supported by historical evidence. Indeed, a quick look back into Afghanistan's history would show that national and international efforts to rapidly develop and modernize Afghan society have tended to fuel political instability rather than stability.[19]

The ultimate failure of foreign-backed development and modernization schemes, including Russian and indigenous communist efforts of decades past, should be readily apparent to today's occupying forces whose bases—from massive facilities like Bagram Air Base and Kandahar Airfield to smaller facilities like Forward Operating Base Chapman, a CIA outpost

---

18   Quoted in Wilder, "Losing Hearts and Minds in Afghanistan," 143.
19   Wilder, "Losing Hearts and Minds in Afghanistan," 144.

near the Pakistani border, and a joint Afghan–ISAF base in the Shinwar district of Afghanistan's Nangarhar Province built during the 2009–2010 "surge"—all occupy the same sites used by Soviet troops. Despite these tangible artifacts of past failures, Washington continues to voice optimism that it can win in Afghanistan while building, quite literally, on the foundations of former foundering foreigners.

Caught between two exceedingly lethal military forces—one that uses suicide bombers and the other employing pilotless, heavily-armed drones—the Afghan people have suffered mightily during the better part of a decade of an American war, that followed harsh Taliban rule after a bloody civil war that itself followed on the heels of a near decade-long Soviet occupation. Even in rare and brief periods of calm, Afghans have seldom found peace, as poverty and privation have left a proud people with little more than the rubble surrounding failed foreign projects that promised prosperity, but ended in the irrigation of uncultivable soil, a leaky and non-functioning hydroelectric power plant, new villages built on arid land, and modern farm machinery, inappropriate to local conditions, left to rust in the fields—all, by the way, themselves artifacts of the joint US–Afghan effort to transform upper Helmand Province and make Marjah into a modern city on a hill in the 1950s.[20]

In the pages that follow, a diverse group of writers from Afghanistan, Pakistan, Russia, the United Kingdom, and the United States—journalists, academics, activists, essayists, and foreign policy experts, including retired US military and CIA personnel, a former British diplomat, a flag officer of the Soviet Navy and even an Afghan interpreter for the US-led International Security Assistance Force—examine myriad facets of the post-2001 US and allied occupation of Afghanistan and a war that has once again brought foreigners to Marjah, as well as so many other towns and villages across Afghanistan where invading armies have long tried to impose their will.

Beginning with selections that offer historical comparisons to, and explore continuities with, Afghanistan's previous occupiers, Great Britain and the Soviet Union, writers of various political persuasions, from committed leftist activists to tough conservative realists, consider such critical issues as the fundamental flaws of US counterinsurgency

---

20   Rohde and Gall, "Mistakes Beset Afghan Project," 35.

doctrine, the failures of efforts to train an effective Afghan Army, the plight of women since the fall of the Taliban, the proliferation of foreign bases inside Afghanistan, "surges" of American troops (as well as CIA operatives and drone strikes), and even evidence of how the United States actually helps to fund its enemy, the Taliban.

By focusing on topics often ignored on the nightly television news and usually far from the front pages of major newspapers, the contributors to *The Case for Withdrawal From Afghanistan* shed light on the most fundamental issues of the conflict. In the process, they expose the many reasons why President Barack Obama's 2009–2010 surge strategy is unlikely to succeed and why it is almost impossible to pinpoint what, exactly, success would look like.

Not all contributors will agree on all points, or even all facts, in this book. Some seek the immediate withdrawal of foreign forces, others see withdrawal as a longer, more complex process. Some believe the United States should have never sent troops to Afghanistan, and others that the time for them to begin to leave has now passed. None have all the answers. Among all of us, there is, however, a core recognition that US and coalition efforts have been deeply flawed and require immediate and intense re-evaluation.

The reasons for this should be obvious. As Jo Comerford, the executive director of the non-profit National Priorities Project has pointed out, Obama's surge is costing American taxpayers $57,077.60 per minute.[21] If the conflict continues over the next ten years, as seems possible, it could cost $1 trillion—on top of the hundreds of billions of dollars already spent on the war since 2001—according to the US Office of Management and Budget. The costs in blood—US, NATO, and Afghan, professional soldier, guerrilla, and civilian—are potentially so much greater. After nearly a decade of conflict, peace and security are nowhere in sight in Afghanistan, and it should be obvious that war is not, and frankly cannot be, the royal road to either of them.

To begin to imagine a true military withdrawal—of troops, bases, and the full-scale machinery of war and occupation—from that country has been the one serious option that has never been put on the proverbial

---

21   Jo Comerford, "$57,077.60: Surging by the Minute," TomDispatch.com, December 17, 2009.

"table" on which "all options" are so regularly said to be placed. It remains on no one's agenda among Washington powerbrokers, and no part of the discussion and debate among its punditocracy or the mainstream media more generally. And yet the situation in Afghanistan calls out for a serious consideration of just that. Laying out the case for real withdrawal is crucial to resolving a war that has long been on the road to perdition. In the pages that follow, all the contributors—some tacitly, some explicitly—set forth evidence that builds a solid case for a foreign troop withdrawal from Afghanistan and the long-overdue need to put the subject of withdrawal on the American agenda.

Nick Turse
New York City
February 2010

Part I THE WARS FOR AFGHANISTAN

1 ARMAGEDDON AT THE TOP OF THE WORLD . . . NOT!: A CENTURY OF FRENZY OVER THE NORTH-WEST FRONTIER

By Juan Cole

WHAT, what, what,
What's the news from Swat?
Sad news,
Bad news,
Comes by the cable led
Through the Indian Ocean's bed,
Through the Persian Gulf, the Red
Sea and the Med-
Iterranean—he's dead;
The Ahkoond is dead!
                    – George Thomas Lanigan

Despite being among the poorest people in the world, the inhabitants of the craggy northwest of what is now Pakistan have managed to throw a series of frights into distant Western capitals for more than a century. That's certainly one for the record books.

And it hasn't ended yet. Not by a long shot. Not with the headlines in the US papers about the depredations of the Pakistani Taliban, not with the CIA's drone aircraft striking gatherings in Waziristan and elsewhere near the Afghan border. In the spring of 2009, for instance, one counter-terrorism analyst stridently (and wholly implausibly) warned that "in one to six months" we could "see the collapse of the Pakistani state" at the hands of the bloodthirsty Taliban, while Secretary of State Hillary Clinton called the situation in Pakistan a "mortal danger" to global security.

What most observers don't realize is that the doomsday rhetoric about this region at the top of the world is hardly new. It's at least a hundred years old. During their campaigns in the northwest in the late nineteenth and early twentieth centuries, British officers, journalists, and editorialists sounded much like American strategists, analysts, and pundits of the present moment. They construed the Pashtun tribesmen who inhabited Waziristan as the new Normans, a dire menace to London that threatened to overturn the British Empire.

The young Winston S. Churchill even wrote a book in 1898, *The Story of the Malakand Field Force*, about a late-nineteenth-century British campaign in Pashtun territory, based on his earlier journalism there. At that time, London ruled British India, comprising all of what is now India, Bangladesh, and Pakistan, but the British hold on the mountainous northwestern region abutting Afghanistan and the Himalayas was tenuous. In trying to puzzle out—like modern analysts—why the predecessors of the Pakistani Taliban posed such a huge challenge to empire, Churchill singled out two reasons for the martial prowess of those Pashtun tribesmen. One was Islam, of which he wrote, "That religion, which above all others was founded and propagated by the sword—the tenets and principles of which are instinct with incentives to slaughter and which in three continents has produced fighting breeds of men—stimulates a wild and merciless fanaticism."

Churchill actually revealed his prejudices here. In fact, for the most part, Islam spread peacefully in what is now Pakistan, by the preaching and poetry of mystical Sufi leaders, and most Muslims have not been more warlike in history than, for example, Anglo-Saxons.

For his second reason, he settled on the environment in which those tribesmen were supposed to thrive. "The inhabitants of these wild but wealthy valleys" are, he explained, in "a continual state of feud and strife." In addition, he insisted, they were early adopters of military technology, so that their weapons were not as primitive as was common among other "races" at what he referred to as "their stage" of development. "To the ferocity of the Zulu are added the craft of the Redskin and the marksmanship of the Boer," he warned.

In these tribesmen, he concluded, "the world is presented with that grim spectacle, 'the strength of civilization without its mercy.'" The Pashtun were, he added, excellent marksmen, who could fell the unwary Westerner with a state-of-the-art breech-loading rifle. "His assailant, approaching, hacks him to death with the ferocity of a South-Sea Islander. The weapons of the nineteenth century are in the hands of the savages of the Stone Age."

Ironically, given Churchill's description of them, when four decades later the Pashtuns joined the freedom movement against British rule that led to the formation of independent Pakistan and India in 1947, politicized Pashtuns were notable not for savagery, but for joining Mahatma Gandhi's campaign of non-violent non-cooperation.

Nevertheless, the Churchillian image of primitive, fanatical brutality armed with cutting-edge technology, which singled Pashtuns out as an extraordinary peril to the West, survived the Victorian era and has now made it into the headlines of our own newspapers. Bruce Riedel, a former CIA analyst, was tasked by the Obama administration to evaluate security threats in Afghanistan and Pakistan. Arnaud de Borchgrave of the *Washington Times* reported breathlessly on July 17, 2009, that Riedel had concluded:

> A jihadist victory in Pakistan, meaning the takeover of the nation by a militant Sunni movement led by the Taliban . . . would create the greatest threat the United States has yet to face in its war on terror . . . [and] is now a real possibility in the foreseeable future.

The article, in true Churchillian fashion, is entitled "Armageddon Alarm Bell Rings."

In fact, few intelligence predictions could have less chance of coming true. In the 2008 parliamentary election, the Pakistani public voted for centrist parties, some of them secular, virtually ignoring the Muslim fundamentalist parties. Today in Pakistan, there are about twenty-four million Pashtuns, a linguistic ethnic group that speaks Pashto. Another thirteen million live across the British-drawn "Durand Line," the border—mostly unacknowledged by Pashtuns—between Pakistan and southern Afghanistan. Most Taliban derive from this group, but the vast majority of Pashtuns are not Taliban and do not much care for the Muslim radicals.

The Taliban force that was handily defeated in the spring of 2009 by the Pakistani army, in a swift campaign in the Swat Valley in the North-West Frontier Province, amounted to a mere 4,000 men. The Pakistani military is 550,000 strong and has a similar number of reservists. It has tanks, artillery, and fighter jets. The Taliban's appeal is limited to that country's Pashtun ethnic group, about 14 percent of the population, and, from everything we can tell, it is a minority taste even among them. The Taliban can commit terrorism and destabilize, but they cannot take over the Pakistani government.

Some Western analysts worry that the Taliban could unite with disgruntled junior officers of the Pakistani Army, who could come to power in a putsch and so offer their Taliban allies access to sophisticated weaponry. Successful Pakistani coups, however, have been made by the chief of staff at the top, not by junior officers, since the military is quite disciplined. Far from coup-making to protect the Taliban, the military has actually spent the past couple of years in hard slogging against them, in the Federally Administered Tribal Area of Bajaur and more recently in Swat.

Today's fantasy of a nuclear-armed Taliban is the modern equivalent of Churchill's anxiety about those all-conquering, ultra-modern Pashtun riflemen with the instincts of savages.

FRONTIER WARD AND WATCH

On a recent research trip to the India Office archives in London to plunge into British military memoirs of the Waziristan campaigns in the first half of the twentieth century, I was overcome by a vivid sense of *déjà vu*. The British in India fought three wars with Afghanistan, losing the first two decisively, and barely achieving a draw in the third in 1919. Among the Afghan king Amanullah's demands during the third war were that the Pashtun tribes of the frontier be allowed to give him their fealty and that Britain permit Afghanistan to conduct a sovereign foreign policy. He lost on the first demand but won on the second, and soon signed a treaty of friendship with the newly established Soviet Union.

Disgruntled Pashtun tribes in Waziristan, a no-man's-land sandwiched between the Afghan border and the formal boundary of the British-ruled North-West Frontier Province, preferred Kabul's rule to that of London and launched their own attacks on the British, beginning in 1919. Putting down the rebellious Wazir and Mahsud tribes of this region would, in the end, cost imperial Britain's treasury three times as much as had the Third Anglo-Afghan War itself.

On May 2, 1921, long after the Pashtun tribesmen should have been pacified, the Manchester *Guardian* carried a panicky news release by the

British Viceroy of India on a Mahsud attack. "Enemy activity continues throughout," the alarmed message from Viceroy Rufus Isaacs, the Marquess of Reading, said, implying that a massive uprising on the subcontinent was under way. In fact, the action at that point was in only a small set of villages in one part of Waziristan, itself but one of several otherwise relatively quiet tribal areas.

On the 23rd of that month, a large band of Mahsud struck "convoys" near the village of Piazha. British losses included a British officer killed, four British and two Indian officers wounded, and seven Indian troops killed, with twenty-six wounded. On the 24th, "a picket [sentry outpost] near Suidgi was ambushed, and lost nine killed and seven wounded." In nearby Zhob, the British received support from friendly Pashtun tribes engaged in a feud with what they called the "hostiles," and—a modern touch—"aeroplanes" weighed in as well. They were, it was said, "cooperating," though this too was an exaggeration. At the time, the Royal Air Force (RAF) was eager to prove its colonial worth on the imperial frontiers in ways that extended beyond simple reconnaissance, even though in 1921 it maintained but a single airplane at Peshawar, the nearest city, which had "a hole in its wing." By 1925, the RAF had gotten its wish and would drop 150 tons of bombs on the Mahsud tribe.

On July 5, 1921, a newspaper report in the Allahabad *Pioneer* gives a sense of the tactics the British deployed against the "hostiles." One center of rebellion was the village of Makin, inhabited by that same Mahsud tribe, which apparently wanted its own irrigation system and freedom from British interference. The British Indian army held the nearby village of Ladka. "Makin was shelled from Ladka on the 20th June," the report ran.

The tribal fighters responded by beginning to move their flocks, though their families remained. British archival sources report that a Muslim holy man, or *faqir*, attempted to give the people of Makin hope by laying a spell on the six-inch howitzer shells and pledging that they would no longer explode in the valley. (Overblown imperial anxiety about such *faqirs* or *akhonds*, Pashtun religious leaders, inspired Victorian satirists such as Edward Lear, who began one poem, "Who, or why, or which, or what,/ Is the Akond of Swat?")

The *faqir*'s spells were to no avail. The shelling, the *Pioneer* reported, continued over the next two days, "with good results." Then, on the 23rd, "another bombardment of Makin was carried out by our 6-inch howitzers at Ladka." This shelling "had a great moral effect," the newspaper intoned, and revealed with satisfaction that "the inhabitants are now evacuating their families." The particular nature of the moral effect of bombarding a civilian village where women and children were known to be present was not explained. Two days later, however, thanks to air observation, the howitzers at Ladka and the guns at "Piazha camp" made a "direct hit" on another similarly obscure village.

Such accounts of small, vicious engagements in mountainous villages with (to British ears) outlandish names fit oddly with the strange conviction of the elite and the press that the fate of the Empire was somehow at stake—just as strangely as similar reports out of exactly the same area, often involving the very same tribes, do in our own time. On July 7, 2009, for instance, the Pakistani newspaper *The Nation* published a typical daily report on the Swat valley campaign which might have come right out of the early twentieth century. Keep in mind that this was a campaign into which the Obama administration forced the Pakistani government to save itself and the American position in the Greater Middle East, and which displaced some two million people, risking the actual destabilization of the whole northwestern region of Pakistan. The report read in part:

> [T]he security forces during search operation at Banjut, Swat, recovered fifty mules loaded with arms and ammunition, medicines and rations and also apprehended a few terrorists. During search operation at Thana, an improvised explosive device (IED) went off causing injuries to a soldier. As a result of operation at Tahirabad, Mingora, the security forces recovered surgical equipment, nine hand grenades and office furniture from the house of a militant.

The unfamiliar place names, the attention to confiscated mules, and the fear of tribal militancy differed little from the reports in the *Pioneer* from nearly a century before. Echoing Viceroy Rufus Isaacs, US Secretary of State Hillary Clinton said on July 14, 2009: "Our national security as well as the future of Afghanistan depends on a stable, democratic, and economically viable Pakistan. We applaud the new Pakistani determination to deal with the militants who threaten their democracy and our shared security."

As in 1921, so in 2009, the skirmishes were ignored by the general public in the West despite the frenzied assertions of politicians that the fate of the world hung in the balance.

A PARANOID VIEW OF THE PASHTUNS, THEN AND NOW

On July 21, 1921, a "correspondent" for the Allahabad *Pioneer*—as anonymous as he was vehement—explained how some firefights in Waziristan might indeed be consequential for Western civilization. He attacked "Irresponsible Criticism" of the military budget required to face down the Mahsud tribe. He asked, "What is India's strategical position in the world today?" It was a leading question. "Along hundreds of miles of her border," he then warned darkly in a mammoth run-on sentence, "are scores of thousands of hardy fighters trained to war and rapine from their very birth, never for an instant forgetful of the soft wealth of India's plains, all of whom would descend to harry them tomorrow if they thought the venture safe, some of whom are determinedly at war with us even now."

Note that he does not explain the challenge posed by the Pashtun tribes in terms of typical military considerations, which would require attention to the exact numbers, training, equipment, tactics, and logistics of the fighters, and which would have revealed them as no significant threat to the Indian plains, however hard they were to control in their own territory. The "correspondent" instead ridicules urban "pen-pushers," who little appreciate the "heavy task" of "frontier ward and watch."

Not only were the tribes a danger in themselves, the hawkish correspondent intoned, but "beyond India's border lies a great country [Afghanistan] with whom we are not even yet technically at peace." Nor was that all. The recently-established Soviet Union, with which Afghanistan had concluded a treaty of friendship that February, loomed as the real threat behind the radical Pashtuns. "Beyond that again is a huge mad-dog nation that acknowledges no right save the sword, no creed save aggression, murder and loot, that will stay at nothing to gain its end, that covets avowedly a descent upon India above all other aims."

That then-Soviet leader Vladimir Lenin, who took an extremely dim view of colonialism and seriously considered freeing the Central Asian possessions of the old Tsarist empire, was then contemplating the rape of India is among the least believable calumnies in imperial propaganda. The "correspondent" would have none of it. Those, he concludes, who dare criticize the military budget should try sweet-talking the Mahsud, the Wazir, and the Bolsheviks.

In our own day as well, pundits configure the uncontrolled Pashtuns as merely the tip of a geostrategic iceberg, with the sinister icy menace of al Qaeda stretching beneath, and beyond that greater challenges to the US such as Iran (incredibly, sometimes charged by the US military with supporting the hyper-Sunni, Shiite-hating Taliban in Afghanistan). Occasionally in this past decade, attempts have even been made to tie the Russian bear once again to the Pashtun tribes.

In the case of the British Empire, whatever the imperial fears, the actual cost in lives and expenditure of campaigning in the Hindu Kush mountain range was enough to ensure that such engagements would be of relatively limited duration. On October 26, 1921, the *Pioneer* reported that the British government of India had determined to implement a new system in Waziristan, dependent on tribal mercenaries.

"This system, which was so successfully inaugurated in the Khyber district last year," the article explained, "is really an adaptation of the methods in vogue forty years ago." The tribal commander provided his own weapons and equipment and, for a fee, protected imperial lines of communication and provided security on the roads. "Thus he has an interest in maintaining the tranquility of his territory, and gives support to the more stable elements among the tribes when the hotheads are apt to run amok." The system would be adopted, the article says, to put an end to the ruinous costs of "punitive expeditions of merely ephemeral pacificatory value."

Absent-minded empire keeps reinventing the local tribal levy, loyal to foreign capitals and paid by them, as a way of keeping the hostiles in check. The US Council on Foreign Relations reported in late 2008 that "US military commanders are studying the feasibility of recruiting Afghan tribesmen . . . to target Taliban and al-Qaeda elements. Taking a page from the so-called 'Sunni Awakening' in Iraq, which turned Sunni tribesmen against militants first in Anbar Province and then beyond, the strategic about-face in Afghanistan would seek to extend power from Kabul to the country's myriad tribal militias." Likewise, the Pakistani government has attempted to deploy tribal fighters against the Taliban in the Federally Administered areas such as Bajaur. It remains to be seen whether this strategy can succeed.

Both in the era between the two world wars and again in the early twenty-first century, the Pashtun peoples have been objects of anxiety in world capitals out of all proportion to the security challenge they actually pose. As it turned out, the real threat to the British Isles in the twentieth century emanated from one of what Churchill called their "civilized" European neighbors. Nothing the British tried in the North-West Frontier and its hinterland actually worked. By the 1940s the British hold on the tribal agencies and frontier regions was shakier than ever before, and the tribes more assertive. After the British were forced out of the subcontinent in 1947, London's anxieties about the Pashtuns and their world-changing potential abruptly evaporated.

Today, we are again hearing that the Waziris and the Mahsuds are dire threats to Western civilization. The tribal struggle for control of obscure villages in the foothills of the Himalayas is being depicted as a life-and-death matter for the North Atlantic world. Again, there is aerial surveillance, bombing, artillery fire, and—this time—displacement of civilians on a scale no British viceroy ever contemplated.

In 1921, vague threats to the British Empire from a small, weak principality of Afghanistan and a nascent, if still supine, Soviet Union underpinned a paranoid view of the Pashtuns. Today, the supposed entanglement with al Qaeda of those Pashtuns termed "Taliban" by US and NATO officials—or even with Iran or Russia—has focused Washington's and Brussels's military and intelligence efforts on the highland villagers once again.

Few of the Pashtuns in question, even the rebellious ones, are really Taliban in the sense of militant seminary students; few so-called Taliban are entwined with what little is left of al Qaeda in the region; and Iran and Russia are not, of course, actually supporting the latter. There may be plausible reasons for which the US and NATO wish to expend blood and treasure in an attempt to forcibly shape the politics of the 38 million Pashtuns on either side of the Durand Line in the twenty-first century. That they form a dire menace to the security of the North Atlantic world is not one of them.

2 THE FAMILIAR ROAD TO FAILURE

By Rodric Braithwaite

On Christmas Day 1979, thirty-one years ago, Soviet forces poured into Afghanistan. Two days later Soviet special forces killed President Hafizullah Amin in his Kabul palace. The Russians imposed their puppet, Babrak Karmal, in his place. Led by Jimmy Carter, the US president, and Margaret Thatcher, the UK prime minister, the world united against this latest example of cynical and ruthless Soviet imperial aggression against a small neighbor. Financial, economic, and military assistance to the growing insurgency flooded in from Pakistan, China, Saudi Arabia, Iran, the US, and Britain. Nine years later, on February 15, 1989, the Soviets withdrew, a superpower humiliated by a rag-tag army of pious peasant fighters armed by US Congressman Charlie Wilson with the Stinger missiles that drove the Soviet battle helicopters out of the sky.

Thus the myth. The reality was more complicated. A good place to start is 1919, when an Afghan army invaded India. The British rapidly defeated them, but in the subsequent peace negotiations they abandoned the eighty-year-old monopoly of Afghan foreign policy for which they had successfully fought in the nineteenth century.

Freed from British tutelage, the Afghans promptly recognized the infant Soviet Union. The Russians had a major, indeed a "legitimate," interest in close links with a country strategically situated on their southern border, a potential source of instability, drugs, Islamic fundamentalism, and American intrigue. They were happy to work with whoever was currently in power in Kabul. They trained Afghan officers and engineers and built many large projects, including a national highway, a strategic road tunnel through the mountains, one of the largest agricultural projects in Asia, and the Polytechnic Institute in Kabul.

By the 1970s they had also developed a close but unhappy relationship with the Afghan communist party, which was fatally split between moderates led by Karmal and extremists led by Nur Mohammed Taraki and Amin. In a bloody coup, to which the Russians were probably not a party, the communists overthrew President Mohammed Daud in April 1978. The extremists then won the factional fight. They believed that the methods pioneered by Stalin could transform Afghanistan into a secular "socialist" country in a matter of years, and began to imprison and execute their opponents in large numbers.

Opposition rapidly spread throughout the country. In March 1978 insurgents, joined by the local garrison, took over the provincial capital of Herat. Stories unbacked by evidence say that up to 100 Soviet advisers and their families were slaughtered.

The Kabul government panicked and appealed to Moscow to send troops. Moscow refused, and Aleksei Kosygin, Soviet prime minister, told Taraki: "We believe it would be a fatal mistake to commit ground troops. If our troops went in, the situation in your country would not improve. On the contrary, it would get worse. Our troops would have to struggle not only with an external aggressor, but with a significant part of your own people." His words were prophetic.

The insurgency went on growing. The Russians continued to turn down repeated Afghan requests for troops. But the Soviet general staff did do some contingency planning, and sent detachments of special forces and paratroopers into Kabul and the air base at Bagram as a precaution.

In the autumn things deteriorated much further. Amin murdered Taraki, took over the country, stepped up the arrests and executions, and began to talk to the Americans. So far, the Russians' attempts to influence the course of Afghan politics had been completely ineffective. Now they feared that the place would slip away from them entirely. They decided something must be done. The KGB made some ineffectual attempts to assassinate Amin. But the military option began to seem unavoidable.

The Russians' objectives were modest. They wanted to stabilize the Afghan government, secure the roads and the main towns, train up the Afghan army and police, and then leave. At that point an argument opened up in Moscow. The politicians agreed with the KGB that a force of 30,000 to 40,000 should be sufficient. The military wanted something much more substantial: they had after all sent some half a million soldiers to invade Czechoslovakia in 1968. The force that finally went into Afghanistan consisted initially of about 80,000 troops. Ironically, Amin believed until the very end that the Russians were coming in response to his repeated requests, and he sent a senior staff officer to the Soviet frontier to smooth their passage.

The 40th Army, as it was called, was inadequate. It was put together in a hurry and, though it grew to about 100,000 men, it was always too small: the military later came to believe that they would have needed thirty-two divisions to subdue Afghanistan and close its border with Pakistan. It was designed to fight on the North German plain, and so was neither equipped nor trained to face an insurgency. The Russian soldiers did eventually learn to fight effectively in the mountains and in what they (and the British soldiers who followed them) called the "green zone," the lethal tangle of booby-trapped irrigation ditches, vineyards, and narrow village streets of the cultivated valleys. But it took time. They lost a lot of people in the process. And they killed a great many Afghans in a war as brutal as the American war in Vietnam.

Two-thirds of the soldiers were engaged in defense: garrisoning the towns, searching villages, manning guard posts along the roads. The aggressive fighting was done by special forces, paratroopers and reconnaissance troops, supported and transported by armored vehicles and helicopters.

Despite their losses, the Russians won most of their fights. They kept the main roads open, something we cannot always do today. They broke mujahideen attempts to besiege cities. They mounted large operations, mustering up to 12,000 troops, to suppress mujahideen bases and formations. They put together an Afghan army, armed with heavy weapons, which often fought well enough, despite the distressing tendency of Afghan officers to change sides and of soldiers to return to their villages when the going got rough.

But the Russians never got over their basic weakness: they could take the territory, but they never had enough troops to hold it. As one Russian critic put it, they had tactics but no strategy.

From the beginning there were critical voices both inside and outside government. The criticism grew as the bodies began to come home in their zinc coffins. People complained bitterly that the war was pointless and shameful, and that their sons were dying in vain. In 1983 the government began to look for an exit strategy. Soon after Mikhail Gorbachev came to power in 1985—well before the first Stinger was fired—he told the Afghans that the Soviet troops would pull out in a year or eighteen months.

That was easier said than done. The Russians needed to save face, to leave a friendly regime behind them, to say that their young men had not died in vain. The mujahideen wanted victory, the Pakistanis wanted to install their allies in Kabul, and the Americans wanted to go on making the Russians bleed in revenge for Vietnam. But after two years of bitter negotiation, the Russians achieved much of what they needed. Their new man, Mohammed Najibullah, remained in control in Kabul, and after nine unsatisfactory years the 40th Army withdrew in good order. Some 15,000 Soviet soldiers had died, and perhaps as many as 1.5 million Afghans.

Najibullah lasted two more years. Then President Boris Yeltsin's new government in Moscow cut off supplies of food, fuel, and weapons, and, like the British puppets of the nineteenth century, he was overthrown and eventually killed. After a vicious civil war, it was left to the Taliban to restore order.

The lessons of history are never clear, and it is risky to predict the future. The British and the Russians won their wars but failed to impose their chosen leaders and systems of government on the Afghans. The Western coalition already has as many troops in Afghanistan as the Russians did, and smarter military technology. But neither the British prime minister nor the generals have explained to us convincingly why we should succeed where the Russians and the British failed, or why fighting in Afghanistan will prevent home-grown fanatics from planting bombs in British cities. Tactics without strategy indeed.

3 AFGHANISTAN, GORKY, AND AN OPEN LETTER TO LEONID BREZHNEV, 1980

By Andrei Sakharov

The USSR sent its troops into Afghanistan in December 1979. A special KGB detachment shot President Hafizullah Amin and everyone who witnessed his execution. In a statement broadcast from Tashkent, Babrak Karmal announced the formation of a new government. That was the beginning for the Soviet army of a protracted war against Afghan guerrillas and, in effect, against the Afghan people.

What purpose did the invasion serve and what have been its consequences? According to Soviet propaganda, the legal government of Afghanistan invited our troops into the country in order to defend the April 1978 revolution against bandits infiltrating from Pakistan. But that explanation is untenable; Amin would hardly have asked for the Soviet troops which were sent to assassinate him. The truth is that Amin's determination to pursue an independent course had made him unacceptable to the Soviet leaders. His domestic policies had provoked serious conflict within the country, but he apparently felt he could manage without outside aid. Armed opposition to both Amin and his predecessor, Nur Mohammed Taraki, who had become president after the 1978 revolution, was for the most part local and tribal; only after the Soviet invasion did resistance become nation-wide and outside assistance for it begin to come in (and then only in small amounts). For Afghans, the consequences of the Soviet intervention were tragic: it brought war and suffering.

The real motive for the invasion was Soviet expansionism. Our leaders may well have been disturbed when the bloody, KGB-assisted overthrow of President Mohammed Daoud in 1978 made Afghanistan less, not more, manageable; but I am convinced that worry about the local situation served only as a pretext for an invasion with far-reaching geopolitical goals, with Afghanistan being regarded as a strategic springboard to Soviet dominance in the surrounding region.

The seizure of the American embassy in Tehran by "revolutionary students" in November 1979, less than two months before the Soviet move into Afghanistan, fractured American–Iranian relations and paved the way for Soviet penetration, playing so smoothly into Soviet hands that one can't help but wonder whether Soviet agents were involved—as foreign press reports suggested.

The Soviet leaders must have been counting on a quick victory in Afghanistan. But this was a country that had in the past fought off both England and Tsarist Russia, and it did not capitulate. As Karmal's army was crippled by mass desertions and defections to the guerrilla forces, the war became steadily more barbaric. We listened with horror and shame to Western broadcasts reporting the bombing of villages, famine caused by the destruction of crops, and the use of napalm, mines, booby traps, and chemical weapons. Four million Afghans, a quarter of the pre-war population, have fled to Pakistan and Iran, where they live in miserable conditions—the largest body of refugees in the world today. Will the Afghans ever forgive the suffering inflicted on them?

During the first months of the war, KGB agents reportedly fired on schoolgirls demonstrating in the streets of Kabul. Crimes like this leave permanent scars. Captured guerrillas are said to have been burned alive, and peasants who aided them executed. The guerrillas themselves are known to have committed atrocities, including savage reprisals against collaborators. One guerrilla spokesman admitted that since they couldn't guard or feed prisoners of war, they shot them. The Soviet forces and their Afghan allies were aware of this practice, but refused to exchange prisoners with the guerrillas; and Soviet helicopters, according to some reports, fired on surrounded Soviet soldiers to prevent their capture.

The invasion of Afghanistan had serious international consequences. It violated that country's non-aligned status, indeed threatened the very concept of non-alignment. It dismayed the Islamic world and placed yet another obstacle in the way of Sino–Soviet rapprochement. The West, the

United States and Japan in particular, viewed the invasion as a dangerous display of Soviet expansionism.

Taken together with other events of that period, the invasion cast doubt on the Soviet Union's respect for international obligations and undermined confidence in its policies and its sincerity in preaching peace and security. This psychological shift led indirectly to improved relations between the West and China, the rethinking of the West's arms program and international strategy, and the US Senate's refusal to ratify the SALT-II Treaty. An overwhelming majority of the UN General Assembly voted to condemn the invasion as a violation of international law, and only a Soviet veto in the Security Council averted the imposition of sanctions.

I am convinced that the invasion was a major blunder, and we don't even know who made the decision or when it was made. Here again, as in Hungary and Czechoslovakia (to say nothing of the 1939 Hitler–Stalin pact), we see the danger posed to the world by a closed, totalitarian society. Westerners ask how Soviet citizens feel about their government's actions in Afghanistan; this question is difficult to answer in the absence of a free press and without public opinion polling on sensitive issues. On the surface, at least, there seems to be astonishing indifference to the true nature of events in Afghanistan, where our sons have become murderers and oppressors—and victims—in a terrible, cruel, dehumanizing war.

As 1980 began, Afghanistan cast a long shadow. Increased latitude was granted to the KGB because of the war and in anticipation of the forthcoming Olympics; this was evidenced in a series of arrests and in my banishment to Gorky. The expansion of the KGB's role was ominous—one "1937" was enough!

OPEN LETTER ON AFGHANISTAN

To the Presidium of the Supreme Soviet of the USSR and to its Chairman, Leonid Brezhnev:

I am sending copies of this letter to the Secretary General of the United Nations and to the heads of state of China, France, the UK, and the US.

I am appealing to you concerning a matter of supreme importance—the situation in Afghanistan. By virtue of my position in the world and as a citizen of the USSR, I feel a responsibility for the tragic events taking place there. I am cognizant of the fact that your point of view is based on information which I am sure is far more comprehensive than that available to me. Nevertheless, the gravity of this question is such that I ask you to give my letter and the opinions expressed in it special attention.

Military operations in Afghanistan have been under way for seven months. Thousands of Soviet and tens of thousands of Afghan citizens have been killed and injured, among them not only Afghan guerrillas, but a great number of civilians in towns and villages—old people, women, and children. More than a million Afghans have become refugees. News of the bombing of villages that assist the guerrillas is extremely ominous, as is the mining of mountain roads, which threatens large regions with starvation. There are reports that napalm, booby traps, and new types of weapons are being used. Reports (unconfirmed) of the use of nerve gas are extremely alarming. Some of this information may be unreliable, but there is no doubt that a terrible situation exists. Escalation of the hostilities and of savagery by both sides continues, and no end is in sight.

The events in Afghanistan have also fundamentally altered the international political situation, jeopardizing peace and détente in this region and throughout the world. They have made more difficult, perhaps even impossible, the ratification of the SALT-II Treaty that is so vital to the entire world, in particular as a necessary first step toward disarmament. Not surprisingly, military budgets have been increased and new military-industrial programs have been approved by all the great powers because of the Soviet actions, and these increases will have long-term ramifications by escalating the danger of an arms race. In the UN General Assembly, 104 countries, including many that have always given unconditional support to the USSR, have denounced the Soviet military operation in Afghanistan.

Supermilitarization of our country, especially disastrous in our difficult economic conditions, is increasing and, as a result, vitally important economic and social reforms are not being implemented. The role of the organs of repression is increasing, and they may easily get out of hand.

I will not analyze in detail the reasons for sending Soviet troops into Afghanistan, whether this was done for legitimate defensive purposes, or as part of some other plan; whether it constituted disinterested assistance for land reform and other social changes, or interference in the internal affairs of a sovereign state. There may be some truth in each of these propositions. I myself believe that the Soviet actions are a clear example of expansionism and are a violation of Afghan sovereignty. But it seems to me that even those who hold a contrary view must agree that these actions are a terrible mistake, one that should be corrected with the greatest possible dispatch, especially since that will become more difficult with each passing day. I am convinced that a political settlement is necessary and that it should include the following measures:

- The USSR and the Afghan guerrillas must cease military operations and sign a truce agreement;
- The USSR must declare its readiness to withdraw all its troops, as soon as they can be replaced by UN forces. This will be a significant action for the UN, in accord with the goals proclaimed at its founding, and with the resolution passed by 104 of its members;
- The permanent members of the UN Security Council (and the countries neighboring Afghanistan) must guarantee the neutrality, peace, and independence of Afghanistan;
- All member states of the United Nations, including the USSR, should offer political asylum to citizens of Afghanistan who wish to leave their country. Freedom of emigration must be one of the terms of the settlement.
- Until elections can be held, the government of Babrak Karmal must transfer its power to a Provisional Council composed of representatives, on a fully equal footing, of both the guerrillas and the Karmal government.

My ideas are meant to serve only as a basis for further discussion. I understand how difficult it may be to implement this program or a similar one, but it is necessary to find a political means to escape from this blind alley. The continuation and, still more, the further escalation of military operations, would, to my mind, lead to disastrous consequences. The world may now be at a crossroads, and the entire course of events in the next few years, even the next few decades, may well depend on the outcome of the Afghan crisis.

July 27, 1980

4 WE WERE WAGING WAR AGAINST A PEOPLE

By Oleg Vasilevich Kustov

In issue forty-six for 2009 of *Nezavisimoe Voennoe Obozrenie* there appeared the recollections of Major General Leonid Shershnev, in which the introduction of Soviet forces into Afghanistan in December 1979 is discussed. I was extraordinarily interested in this material, since I myself was a participant in those events.

Unfortunately, the contents of what I read disappointed me in equally extraordinary fashion. Anyone familiar with Major General Shershnev's memoirs might conclude that our Afghan campaign possessed not a trace of tragedy, and that the path of Soviet soldiers on foreign soil was scattered with rose petals.

We need to begin with the fact that, in its very essence, the decision to send troops into Afghanistan and to eliminate Amin was criminal from the point of view of international law, as well as all moral and ethical norms common to humanity. The decision had fateful consequences for both the Soviet Union and Afghanistan, as well as for the peoples of both countries. It is as if someone in the Soviet leadership could not rest in face of the "laurels" won by the French, British, and especially Americans, who—to satisfy their ambitions and selfish interests—change regimes as if they were gloves in Latin America, Africa, the Near and Middle East, and Southeast Asia, taking no account of any norms laid down in international obligations, the UN Charter, and so on.

Now let us return to the events directly connected with the introduction of Soviet forces into Afghanistan—the liquidation of Amin and the installation in power of Moscow's placeman Babrak Karmal with his comrades.

Soviet divisions entered the DRA[1] simultaneously from two directions, in one case making use of a pontoon bridge across the Amu-Darya near the Afghan river-port of Khairaton. A curious detail. In 1989, when the last column of the 40th Army, led by its commanding officer General Boris Gromov, crossed back into Soviet territory from Afghanistan across a fixed bridge, one of our TV journalists solemnly announced that it was precisely across this bridge that "our forces entered Afghanistan, and are now leaving it." But this road and rail bridge, named Friendship Bridge, was only built more than three years after our arrival in Afghanistan.

In 1979 our intervention also took place across the border in the region of Kushka, in the direction of Herat, and also by air, with military transport aircraft flying to the aerodrome in Kabul and the airbase at Bagram. The planes delivered elements, materiel, and stores for airborne and special forces units of the KGB and GRU.[2] Moreover, forces were in fact being introduced under the propaganda cover of repeated requests from the Afghan leadership, beginning with Taraki, for help for the government of the DRA in its battle with "insurgents." It is significant that on the day of the operation against Amin, the latter was planning to appear on television with an appeal to the people on precisely this point, but did not receive confirmation on the text from the Soviet leadership, for reasons that will, I am sure, be obvious to readers.

At the time there were very few people who realized what colossal, unjustifiable losses for the Soviet Union—political, economic, moral, psychological, material, and human—would result from this action. Any honest person who has had something to do with Afghanistan has lodged in their soul, like a splinter, these questions: In the name of what, and why, did more than 13,000 of our soldiers die and were over 100,000 physically maimed? Why did the majority of the hundreds of thousands of soldiers and officers who went through "Afghan" become "superfluous people" on their return to the USSR, many of them in their hardship turning to crime?

I have heard one version of how the decision on Afghanistan was taken. I was told that "dear Leonid Ilyich" was sorely offended by Amin giving the

---

1   Democratic Republic of Afghanistan. *Editor's note.*

2   Glavnoye Razvedyvatel'noye Upravleniye, Soviet military intelligence. *Editor's note.*

order to suffocate Taraki, head of the Central Committee of the PDPA[3] after the April 1978 coup. The latter stopped in Moscow on his way back from a conference of non-aligned countries in Havana, was warmly received, and, according to the Soviet tradition of those times, exchanged kisses with Leonid Ilyich; the large photographs that appeared in all the Soviet and Afghan newspapers testify to this. It's not impossible that this actually happened. Under Leonid Brezhnev, all manner of things were possible. He himself received the Order of Victory and had the military rank of Marshal of the Soviet Union, as well as receiving the Lenin Prize for "outstanding achievements" in the field of literature.

The main tragedy of the situation consisted in the fact that the overwhelming majority of participants in those events had no idea or any information about the reasons for the decision taken by the political leadership of the USSR. It was explained to soldiers and officers that they were going to Afghanistan in order to provide "assistance to the Afghan people," to "fulfill an international duty" in the struggle against mercenaries and mutineers, and to "thwart the attempts of the imperialists" to overthrow the revolutionary regime of the DRA.

Naturally, everyone was convinced that Soviet soldiers would be received as friends in Afghanistan. The reality turned out to be very far from the ideological postulates the authorities tried to instill in our soldiers. The majority of the country's population met us as foes, and saw us off as sworn enemies. During the whole period in which the "limited contingent of Soviet forces" was on Afghan soil, between 5 and 10 percent of the territory was under the control of "the people's power" (read: Soviet control). Even in the capital, Kabul, in most districts it was dangerous to go more than 200 or 300 meters from installations guarded by our troops or detachments of the Afghan army, internal forces, and secret services—to do so was to put one's life at risk. To be completely honest, we were waging war against a people.

Illusions that we would be met as friends resulted in tragedy for many of our detachments, especially in the early period of their stay in Afghan territory. A number of incidents were recorded in which Soviet soldiers were offered hospitality, and killed with astonishing cruelty. The author has had occasion to read the conclusions of the medical examiners on the savagely

---

3   People's Democratic Party of Afghanistan. *Editor's note.*

cruel killings of his compatriots. Their eyes were gouged out, their throats slit, their hands, feet, and sexual organs were cut off, their bellies were ripped open and body parts placed inside them. Such incidents took place not only with Soviet military personnel, but also with civilian specialists. The first such outrage took place at the beginning of 1979 during a revolt in Herat, long before the introduction of Soviet troops. A second, analogous crime took place on December 31, 1979, in Kandahar, where three Soviet civilian specialists, who had been working on repairs to equipment in a textile factory we were building there, were brutally killed. As later became clear, the majority of the fifteen Soviet citizens working there had expressed doubts about a trip [to Kandahar] to buy food for a New Year's dinner, to which the leader of the group categorically objected, declaring, "We're bringing the Afghans peace and the possibility of work, so nothing is going to happen to us!"

There was another illusion, based on a belief in the propagandistic assertions of the Soviet leadership. It was thought that detachments of Soviet troops sent into Afghanistan should contain as many people as possible from the Central Asian republics of the USSR—Tajiks, Uzbeks, Kyrgyz, Turkmens, Kazakhs. Even the designated "Muslim" battalion of GRU special forces that stormed Amin's palace was composed principally of them.

The scales began to fall from the eyes of our leadership fairly rapidly when the representatives of Soviet national minorities often pretended to fight but then started to fraternize with the mujahideen and go over to their side. Some of the deserters continued to take part in combat operations against our soldiers on the side of those whom we called "counter-revolutionaries" right up until the withdrawal of Soviet troops from Afghanistan.

Meanwhile the transport of our forces to Kabul by air began in tragedy: a Il-76 military transport aircraft, due to poor knowledge of the physical relief of the local landscape and the particularities of landing at the aerodrome of the Afghan capital, which had practically no radio equipment, crashed into a mountain. On board the plane were a fully loaded petrol tanker and more than thirty men. More people died in this catastrophe than in the entire operation to seize Amin's palace, the ministries, and government departments in Kabul. Afterwards, Il-76s were replaced by giant An-22s, and additional measures were taken on the organization of landing and take-off of our planes at the capital's airport.

To this day, the roar of the transporters' engines, which did not cease for three days, rings in the ears of witnesses to those events. The memory also remains of the total incomprehension and perplexity on the part of the representatives of the military leadership, ministries, and government structures of the DRA, and also of our numerous advisers and specialists working within these structures, with regard to what was actually happening. I think that the absolute majority of our soldiers who were led into Afghanistan found themselves in a similar position.

LESSONS NOT LEARNED

The absence of the required level of information and the extraordinary secrecy surrounding everything related to the events of the end of December 1979 led to a series of sad, and sometimes comical, consequences. In particular, the operation to seize Amin's palace, the ministries of defense and the interior, communications, radio and television, the security services, and Kabul airport turns out to have been very poorly organized from a military-medical point of view. Whoever took the decision probably assumed that there would be no losses at all on our side. In reality the outcome was that there was practically no one to assist the wounded, and nothing to assist them with.

From Amin's palace to the USSR embassy is a little more than two kilometers. On the grounds of our diplomatic delegation there was the hospital of the staff of the economic adviser in Kabul, the head doctor of which was Aleksandr Sergeevich Borisov, a highly qualified traumatologist and surgeon. When the first wounded began to arrive, it turned out that the hospital did not have enough painkillers, dressings, antiseptics or specialists who could receive those injured in battle, carry out the necessary operations, and care for them.

Borisov broadcast an appeal over the embassy radio for all those who had medical training to gather as many medications as possible from domestic pharmacies, sterilize sheets and tear them into bandages, and urgently come to the hospital to help him look after the wounded. Borisov, who sadly later died tragically, in practice took all this on his own shoulders—and incidentally, received not a single state honor for it.

But what would it have cost, without giving Aleksandr Sergeevich knowledge of the essence of the operation, to prepare all the necessary equipment, which would have allowed medical aid to have been organized by qualified people?

A difficult task was at the very last moment placed on the shoulders of officers from the staff of our main military adviser. They were tasked with persuading the officers of all levels in the armed forces of the DRA to give the order to their men to lay down their weapons and offer no resistance to Soviet detachments. In the majority of cases they were successful. In particular, at the Kabul aerodrome the Afghans only once opened fire—and that accidentally—on an armored vehicle of the airborne troops. Only one man died as a result. If the attempts at persuasion by our advisers led to nothing, as for example in the case of the head of the general staff, Afghan generals and officers were simply eliminated.

Paradoxical as it may seem, when the sending of troops into Afghanistan was planned, the climatic conditions of the mountains and possibilities for providing Soviet military personnel with food were not given the consideration they should have been. In December and January around Kabul the air temperature varies between minus twenty degrees at night to plus ten during the day, while near the Salang Tunnel it drops as low as minus thirty. Our troops, including the 108th Motorized Rifle Division, which Major General [Leonid] Shershnev discusses in his memoirs, did not even have heated tents.

But tents were the least of it! To begin with we had to bring firewood in planes from Tashkent. And only after a certain time were detachments provided with metal stoves of the kind known since the Russian Civil War as *burzhuiki* ("bourgeois"), which burnt not wood but—like the "uncivilized Afghans" did with their stoves—diesel fuel with a special dosing mechanism dispensing droplets, which allowed them to be used economically.

A similar situation applied to food supplies. Within a couple of days of the arrival of Soviet forces in Kabul, nearly all the meat had been bought up in the capital's markets. The next day, meat prices rose three- or fourfold, after which, on a recommendation from the Soviet trade representative and ambassador, units of the 40th Army were forbidden from buying food from the local population.

In areas where detachments of our forces were deployed, including those located near army headquarters (which was in the actual Taj-Bek Palace), there were no roads, and the earth was covered with impassable mud, which would have been difficult to get through even with army of UAZ cross-country vehicles. It was only afterwards, a year or two later, that areas where the Soviet "limited contingent" was deployed were set up as they should have been, with barracks and other accommodations as well as warehouses being put up, roads extended, helipads built, and so on. All of this was handed over by Soviet forces before their withdrawal from the DRA to units of the armed forces of Afghanistan.

Unfortunately, a large number of Soviet soldiers were buried with monuments and obelisks on the territory of that long-suffering country. I think that for a long time now, nothing has remained of them.

In sum, everything that happened in that period, including the real reasons (the reasons, that is, rather than the grounds given) for the introduction of Soviet forces into Afghanistan, deserves separate, serious investigation. After all, the archives contain all the correspondence between the embassy, the offices of the main military adviser, the economic adviser, the trade representative, the command of the 40th Army, and the representatives of the KGB and MVD[4] with their departments and "higher instance," which implied the structures of the Central Committee of the CPSU. This should have been done long ago. Then it would have been possible to avoid many errors and mistakes that were soon repeated in the hotspots of the Soviet Union as it fell apart, in Chechnya, and in other republics of the North Caucasus.

---

4   Ministerstvo Vnutrennikh Del, the Soviet Ministry of Internal Affairs. *Editor's note.*

5 ABOLISH THE CIA!

By Chalmers Johnson

Steve Coll ends his important book on Afghanistan, *Ghost Wars: The Secret History of the CIA*, by quoting Afghan President Hamid Karzai: "What an unlucky country." Americans might find this a convenient way to ignore what their government did in Afghanistan between 1979 and the present, but luck had nothing to do with it. Brutal, incompetent, secret operations of the US Central Intelligence Agency, frequently manipulated by the military intelligence agencies of Pakistan and Saudi Arabia, caused the catastrophic devastation of this poor country. On the evidence contained in Coll's books, neither the Americans nor their victims in numerous Muslim and Third World countries will ever know peace until the Central Intelligence Agency has been abolished.

It should by now be generally accepted that the Soviet invasion of Afghanistan on Christmas Eve 1979 was deliberately provoked by the United States. In his memoir published in 1996, the former CIA director Robert Gates made it clear that the American intelligence services began to aid the mujahideen guerrillas not after the Soviet invasion, but six months before it. In an interview two years later with *Le Nouvel Observateur*, President Carter's national security adviser Zbigniew Brzezinski proudly confirmed Gates's assertion. "According to the official version of history," Brzezinski said, "CIA aid to the mujahideen began during 1980, that's to say, after the Soviet army invaded Afghanistan. But the reality, kept secret until now, is completely different: on July 3, 1979, President Carter signed the first directive for secret aid to the opponents of the pro-Soviet regime in Kabul. And on the same day, I wrote a note to the president in which I explained that in my opinion this aid would lead to a Soviet military intervention."

Asked whether he in any way regretted these actions, Brzezinski replied: "Regret what? The secret operation was an excellent idea. It drew the Russians into the Afghan trap and you want me to regret it? On the day that the Soviets officially crossed the border, I wrote to President Carter, saying, in essence: 'We now have the opportunity of giving to the USSR its Vietnam War.' "

> *Nouvel Observateur*: And neither do you regret having supported Islamic fundamentalism, which has given arms and advice to future terrorists?
> *Brzezinski*: What is more important in world history? The Taliban or the collapse of the Soviet empire? Some agitated Muslims or the liberation of Central Europe and the end of the Cold War?

Even though the demise of the Soviet Union owes more to Mikhail Gorbachev than to Afghanistan's partisans, Brzezinski certainly helped produce "agitated Muslims," and the consequences have been obvious ever since. Carter, Brzezinski, and their successors in the Reagan and first Bush administrations, including Gates, Dick Cheney, Donald Rumsfeld, Condoleezza Rice, Paul Wolfowitz, Richard Armitage, and Colin Powell, all bear some responsibility for the 1.8 million Afghan casualties, 2.6 million refugees, and 10 million unexploded landmines that followed from their decisions. They must also share the blame for the blowback that struck New York and Washington on September 11, 2001. After all, al Qaeda was an organization they helped create and arm.

A WIND BLOWS IN FROM AFGHANISTAN

The term "blowback" first appeared in a classified CIA post-action report on the overthrow of the Iranian government in 1953, carried out in the interests of British Petroleum. In 2000, James Risen of the *New York Times* explained: "When the Central Intelligence Agency helped overthrow Muhammad Mossadegh as Iran's prime minister in 1953, ensuring another twenty-five years of rule for Shah Muhammad Reza Pahlavi, the CIA was already figuring that its first effort to topple a foreign government would not be its last. The CIA, then just six years old and deeply committed to winning the Cold War, viewed its covert action in Iran as a blueprint for coup plots elsewhere around the world, and so commissioned a secret history to detail for future generations of CIA operatives how it had been done . . . Amid the sometimes curious argot of the spy world—'safebases' and 'assets' and the like—the CIA warns of the possibilities of 'blowback'. The word . . . has since come into use as shorthand for the unintended consequences of covert operations."

"Blowback" does not refer simply to reactions to historical events, but more specifically to reactions to operations carried out by the US government that are kept secret from the American public and from most of their representatives in Congress. This means that when civilians become victims of a retaliatory strike, they are at first unable to put it in context or to understand the sequence of events that led up to it. Even though the American people may not know what has been done in their name, those on the receiving end certainly do: they include the people of Iran (1953), Guatemala (1954), Cuba (1959 to the present), Congo (1960), Brazil (1964), Indonesia (1965), Vietnam (1961–73), Laos (1961–73), Cambodia (1969–73), Greece (1967–73), Chile (1973), Afghanistan (1979 to the present), El Salvador, Guatemala and Nicaragua (1980s), and Iraq (1991 to the present). Not surprisingly, sometimes these victims try to get even.

There is a direct line between the attacks on September 11, 2001—the most significant instance of blowback in the history of the CIA—and the events of 1979. In that year, revolutionaries threw both the Shah and the Americans out of Iran, and the CIA, with full presidential authority, began its largest ever clandestine operation: the secret arming of Afghan freedom fighters to wage a proxy war against the Soviet Union, which involved the recruitment and training of militants from all over the Islamic world. Steve Coll's book is a classic study of blowback and is a better, fuller reconstruction of this history than the findings of *The National Commission on Terrorist Attacks upon the United States* (the "9/11 Commission Report").

From 1989 to 1992, Coll was the *Washington Post*'s South Asia bureau chief, based in New Delhi. Given the CIA's paranoid and often self-defeating secrecy, what makes his book especially interesting is how he came to know what he claims to know. He has read everything on the Afghan insurgency and the civil wars that followed, and has been given access to the original manuscript of Robert Gates's memoir (Gates was the CIA director from 1991 to 1993), but his main source is some 200 interviews conducted between the autumn of 2001 and the summer of 2003 with numerous CIA officials as well as politicians, military officers, and spies from all the countries involved except Russia. He identifies CIA officials only if their names have already been made public. Many of his most important interviews were on the record, and he quotes from them extensively.

Among the notable figures who agreed to be interviewed were Benazir Bhutto, who was candid about having lied to American officials for two years about Pakistan's aid to the Taliban, and Anthony Lake, the US national security adviser from 1993 to 1997, who let it be known that he thought CIA director James Woolsey was "arrogant, tin-eared and brittle." Woolsey was so disliked by Clinton that when an apparent suicide pilot crashed a single-engine Cessna airplane on the south lawn of the White House in 1994, jokers suggested it might be the CIA director trying to get an appointment with the president.

Among the CIA people who talked to Coll are Gates; Woolsey; Howard Hart, Islamabad station chief in 1981; Clair George, former head of clandestine operations; William Piekney, Islamabad station chief from 1984 to 1986; Cofer Black, Khartoum station chief in the mid-1990s and director of the Counterterrorist Center from 1999 to 2002; Fred Hitz, a former CIA Inspector General; Thomas Twetten, Deputy Director of Operations, 1991–1993; Milton Bearden, chief of station at Islamabad, 1986–1989; Duane R. "Dewey" Clarridge, head of the Counterterrorist Center from 1986 to 1988; Vincent Cannistraro, an officer in the Counterterrorist Center shortly after it was opened in 1986; and an official Coll identifies only as "Mike," the head of the "bin Laden Unit" within the Counterterrorist Center from 1997 to 1999, who was subsequently revealed to be Michael F. Scheuer, the anonymous author of *Imperial Hubris: Why the West Is Losing the War on Terror*.

In 1973, General Sardar Mohammed Daoud, the cousin and brother-in-law of King Zahir Shah, overthrew the king, declared Afghanistan a republic, and instituted a program of modernization. Zahir Shah went into exile in Rome. These developments made possible the rise of the People's Democratic Party of Afghanistan, a pro-Soviet communist party, which, in early 1978, with extensive help from the USSR, overthrew President Daoud. The communists' policies of secularization in turn provoked a violent response from devout Islamists. The anti-communist revolt that began at Herat in western Afghanistan in March 1979 originated in a government initiative to teach girls to read. The fundamentalist Afghans opposed to this were supported by a triumvirate of nations—the US, Pakistan, and Saudi Arabia—with quite diverse motives, but the US didn't take these differences seriously until it was too late. By the time the Americans woke up, at the end of the 1990s, the radical Islamist Taliban had established its government in Kabul. Recognized only by Pakistan, Saudi Arabia, and the United Arab

Emirates, it granted Osama bin Laden freedom of action and offered him protection from American efforts to capture or kill him.

Coll concludes: "The Afghan government that the United States eventually chose to support beginning in the late autumn of 2001—a federation of Ahmed Shah Massoud's organization [the Northern warlords], exiled intellectuals and royalist Pashtuns—was available for sponsorship a decade before, but the United States could not see a reason then to challenge the alternative, radical Islamist vision promoted by Pakistani and Saudi intelligence . . . Indifference, lassitude, blindness, paralysis and commercial greed too often shaped American foreign policy in Afghanistan and South Asia during the 1990s."

FUNDING THE FUNDAMENTALISTS

The motives of the White House and the CIA were shaped by the Cold War: a determination to kill as many Soviet soldiers as possible and the desire to restore some aura of rugged machismo as well as credibility that US leaders feared they had lost when the Shah of Iran was overthrown. The CIA had no intricate strategy for the war it was unleashing in Afghanistan. Howard Hart, the Agency's representative in the Pakistani capital, told Coll that he understood his orders as: "You're a young man; here's your bag of money, go raise hell. Don't fuck it up, just go out there and kill Soviets." These orders came from a most peculiar American. William Casey, the CIA's director from January 1981 to January 1987, was a Catholic Knight of Malta educated by Jesuits. Statues of the Virgin Mary filled his mansion, called "Maryknoll," on Long Island. He attended mass daily and urged Christianity on anyone who asked his advice. Once settled as CIA director under Reagan, he began to funnel covert action funds through the Catholic Church to anti-communists in Poland and Central America, sometimes in violation of American law. He believed fervently that by increasing the Catholic Church's reach and power he could contain communism's advance, or reverse it. From Casey's convictions grew the most important US foreign policies of the 1980s—support for an international anti-Soviet crusade in Afghanistan and sponsorship of state terrorism in Nicaragua, El Salvador, and Guatemala.

Casey knew next to nothing about Islamic fundamentalism or the grievances of Middle Eastern nations against Western imperialism. He saw political Islam and the Catholic Church as natural allies in the counter-strategy of covert action to thwart Soviet imperialism. He believed that the USSR was trying to strike at the US in Central America and in the oil-producing states of the Middle East. He supported Islam as a counter to the Soviet Union's atheism, and Coll suggests that he sometimes conflated lay Catholic organizations such as Opus Dei with the Muslim Brotherhood, the Egyptian extremist organization, of which Ayman al-Zawahiri, Osama bin Laden's chief lieutenant, was a passionate member. The Muslim Brotherhood's branch in Pakistan, the Jamaat-i-Islami, was strongly backed by the Pakistani army, and Coll writes that Casey, more than any other American, was responsible for welding the alliance of the CIA, Saudi intelligence, and the army of General Mohammed Zia-ul-Haq, Pakistan's military dictator from 1977 to 1988. On the suggestion of the Pakistani Inter-Services Intelligence (ISI) organization, Casey went so far as to print thousands of copies of the Koran, which he shipped to the Afghan frontier for distribution in Afghanistan and Soviet Uzbekistan. He also fomented, without presidential authority, Muslim attacks inside the USSR and always held that the CIA's clandestine officers were too timid. He preferred the type represented by his friend Oliver North.

Over time, Casey's position hardened into CIA dogma, which its agents, protected by secrecy from ever having their ignorance exposed, enforced in every way they could. The Agency resolutely refused to help choose winners and losers among the Afghan jihad's guerrilla leaders. The result, according to Coll, was that "Zia-ul-Haq's political and religious agenda in Afghanistan gradually became the CIA's own." In the era after Casey, some scholars, journalists, and members of Congress questioned the Agency's lavish support of the Pakistan-backed Islamist general Gulbuddin Hekmatyar, especially after he refused to shake hands with Ronald Reagan because he was an infidel. But Milton Bearden, the Islamabad station chief from 1986 to 1989, and Frank Anderson, chief of the Afghan task force at Langley, vehemently defended Hekmatyar on the grounds that "he fielded the most effective anti-Soviet fighters."

Even after the Soviet Union withdrew from Afghanistan in 1988, the CIA continued to follow Pakistani initiatives, such as aiding Hekmatyar's successor, Mullah Omar, leader of the Taliban. When Edmund McWilliams, the State Department's special envoy to the Afghan resistance in 1988–1989, wrote that "American authority and billions of dollars in taxpayer funding had been hijacked at the war's end by a ruthless anti-American cabal of Islamists and Pakistani intelligence officers determined to impose their will on Afghanistan," CIA officials denounced him and planted stories in the embassy that he might be homosexual or an alcoholic. Meanwhile, Afghanistan descended into one of the most horrific civil wars of the twentieth century. The CIA never fully corrected its naive and ill-informed reading of Afghan politics until after bin Laden bombed the US embassies in Nairobi and Dar es Salaam on August 7, 1998.

FAIR-WEATHER FRIENDS

A cooperative agreement between the US and Pakistan was anything but natural or based on mutual interests. Only two weeks after radical students seized the American Embassy in Tehran on November 5, 1979, a similar group of Islamic radicals burned to the ground the American Embassy in Islamabad as Zia's troops stood idly by. But the US was willing to overlook almost anything the Pakistani dictator did in order to keep him committed to the anti-Soviet jihad. After the Soviet invasion, Brzezinski wrote to Carter: "This will require a review of our policy toward Pakistan, more guarantees to it, more arms aid, and, alas, a decision that our security policy toward Pakistan cannot be dictated by our non-proliferation policy." History will record whether Brzezinski made an intelligent decision in giving a green light to Pakistan's development of nuclear weapons in return for assisting the anti-Soviet insurgency.

Pakistan's motives in Afghanistan were very different from those of the US. Zia was a devout Muslim and a passionate supporter of Islamist groups in his own country, in Afghanistan, and throughout the world. But he was not a fanatic and had some quite practical reasons for supporting Islamic radicals in Afghanistan. He probably would not have been included in the US Embassy's annual "beard census" of Pakistani military officers, which recorded the number of officer graduates and serving generals who kept their beards in accordance with Islamic traditions as an unobtrusive measure of increasing or declining religious radicalism—Zia had only a mustache.

From the beginning, Zia demanded that all weapons and aid for the Afghans from whatever source pass through ISI hands. The CIA was delighted to agree. Zia feared above all that Pakistan would be squeezed between a Soviet-dominated Afghanistan and a hostile India. He also had to guard against a Pashtun independence movement that, if successful, would break up Pakistan. In other words, he backed the Islamic militants in Afghanistan and Pakistan on religious grounds but was quite prepared to use them strategically. In doing so, he laid the foundations for Pakistan's anti-Indian insurgency in Kashmir in the 1990s.

Zia died in a mysterious plane crash on August 17, 1988, four months after the signing of the Geneva Accords on April 14, 1988, which ratified the formal terms of the Soviet withdrawal from Afghanistan. As the Soviet troops departed, Hekmatyar embarked on a clandestine plan to eliminate his rivals and establish his Islamic party, dominated by the Muslim Brotherhood, as the most powerful national force in Afghanistan. The US scarcely paid attention, but continued to support Pakistan. With the fall of the Berlin Wall in 1989 and the implosion of the USSR in 1991, the US lost virtually all interest in Afghanistan. Hekmatyar was never as good as the CIA thought he was, and with the creation in 1994 of the Taliban, both Pakistan and Saudi Arabia transferred their secret support. This new group of jihadis proved to be the most militarily effective of the warring groups. On September 26, 1996, the Taliban conquered Kabul. The next day they killed the formerly Soviet-backed President Najibullah, expelled 8,000 female undergraduate students from Kabul University, and fired a similar number of women schoolteachers. As the mujahideen closed in on his palace, Najibullah told reporters: "If fundamentalism comes to Afghanistan, war will continue for many years. Afghanistan will turn into a center of world smuggling for narcotic drugs. Afghanistan will be turned into a center for terrorism." His comments would prove all too accurate.

Pakistan's military intelligence officers hated Benazir Bhutto, Zia's elected successor, but she, like all post-Zia heads of state including General Pervez Musharraf, supported the Taliban in pursuit of Zia's "dream"—a loyal, Pashtun-led Islamist government in Kabul. Coll explains:

> Every Pakistani general, liberal or religious, believed in the jihadists by 1999, not from personal Islamic conviction, in most cases, but because the jihadists had proved themselves over many years as the one force able to frighten, flummox and bog down the Hindu-dominated Indian army. About a dozen Indian divisions had been tied up in Kashmir during the late 1990s to suppress a few thousand well-trained, paradise-seeking Islamist guerrillas. What more could Pakistan ask? The jihadist guerrillas were a more practical day-to-day strategic defense against Indian hegemony than even a nuclear bomb. To the west, in Afghanistan, the Taliban provided geopolitical "strategic depth" against India

and protection from rebellion by Pakistan's own restive Pashtun population. For Musharraf, as for many other liberal Pakistani generals, jihad was not a calling, it was a professional imperative. It was something he did at the office. At quitting time he packed up his briefcase, straightened the braid on his uniform, and went home to his normal life.

If the CIA understood any of this, it never let on to its superiors in Washington, and Charlie Wilson, a highly paid Pakistani lobbyist and former congressman for East Texas (who "used his trips to the Afghan frontier in part to impress upon a succession of girlfriends how powerful he was"), was anything but forthcoming with Congress about what was really going on. During the 1980s, Wilson had used his power on the House Appropriations Committee to supply all the advanced weapons the CIA might want in Afghanistan. Coll remarks that Wilson "saw the mujahidin through the prism of his own whisky-soaked romanticism, as noble savages fighting for freedom, as almost biblical figures."

ENTER BIN LADEN AND THE SAUDIS

Saudi Arabian motives were different from those of both the US and Pakistan. Saudi Arabia is, after all, the only modern nation-state created by jihad. The Saudi royal family, which came to power at the head of a movement of Wahhabi religious fundamentalists, espoused Islamic radicalism in order to keep it under their control, at least domestically. "Middle-class, pious Saudis flush with oil wealth," Coll writes, "embraced the Afghan cause as American churchgoers might respond to an African famine or a Turkish earthquake": "The money flowing from the kingdom arrived at the Afghan frontier in all shapes and sizes: gold jewelry dropped on offering plates by merchants' wives in Jedda mosques; bags of cash delivered by business-men to Riyadh charities as zakat, an annual Islamic tithe; fat checks written from semi-official government accounts by minor Saudi princes; bountiful proceeds raised in annual telethons led by Prince Salman, the governor of Riyadh." Richest of all were the annual transfers from the Saudi General Intelligence Department, or Istakhbarat, to the CIA's Swiss bank accounts.

From the moment Agency money and weapons started to flow to the mujahideen in late 1979, Saudi Arabia matched the US payments dollar for dollar. They also bypassed the ISI and supplied funds directly to the groups in Afghanistan they favored, including the one led by their own pious young millionaire, Osama bin Laden. According to the CIA's Milton Bearden, private Saudi and Arab funding of up to $25 million a month flowed to Afghan Islamist armies. Equally important, Pakistan trained between 16,000 and 18,000 fresh Muslim recruits on the Afghan frontier every year, and another 6,500 or so were instructed by Afghans inside the country beyond ISI control. Most of these eventually joined bin Laden's private army of 35,000 "Arab Afghans."

Much to the confusion of the Americans, moderate Saudi leaders, such as Prince Turki, the intelligence chief, supported the Saudi backing of funda-mentalists so long as they were in Afghanistan and not in Saudi Arabia. A graduate of a New Jersey prep school and a member of Bill Clinton's class of 1964 at Georgetown University, Turki belonged to the pro-Western, modernizing wing of the Saudi royal family. But that did not make him pro-American. Turki saw Saudi Arabia in continual competition with its powerful Shia neighbor, Iran. He needed credible Sunni, pro-Saudi Islamist clients to compete with Iran's clients, especially in countries like Pakistan and Afghanistan, which have sizeable Shia populations.

Prince Turki was also irritated by the US loss of interest in Afghanistan after its Cold War skirmish with the Soviet Union. He understood that the US would ignore Saudi aid to Islamists so long as his country kept oil prices under control and cooperated with the Pentagon on the building of military bases. Like many Saudi leaders, Turki probably underestimated the longer-term threat of Islamic militancy to the Saudi royal house, but, as Coll observes, "Prince Turki and other liberal princes found it easier to appease their domestic Islamist rivals by allowing them to proselytize and make mischief abroad than to confront and resolve these tensions at home." In Riyadh, the CIA made almost no effort to recruit paid agents or collect intelligence. The result was that Saudi Arabia worked continuously to enlarge the ISI's proxy jihad forces in both Afghanistan and Kashmir, and the Saudi Ministry for the Propagation of Virtue and the Prevention of Vice, the kingdom's religious police, tutored and supported the Taliban's own Islamic police force.

By the late 1990s, after the embassy bombings in East Africa, the CIA and the White House awoke to the Islamist threat, but they defined it almost exclusively in terms of Osama bin Laden's leadership of al Qaeda and failed to see the larger context. They did not target the Taliban, Pakistani military intelligence, or the funds flowing to the Taliban and al Qaeda from Saudi

Arabia and the United Arab Emirates. Instead, they devoted themselves to trying to capture or kill bin Laden. Coll's chapters on the hunt for the al Qaeda leader are entitled, "You Are to Capture Him Alive," "We Are at War," and "Is There Any Policy?" but he might more accurately have called them "Keystone Kops" or "The Gang that Couldn't Shoot Straight."

On February 23, 1998, bin Laden summoned newspaper and TV reporters to the camp at Khost that the CIA had built for him at the height of the anti-Soviet jihad. He announced the creation of a new organization—the International Islamic Front for Jihad against Jews and Crusaders—and issued a manifesto saying that "to kill and fight Americans and their allies, whether civilian or military, is an obligation for every Muslim who is able to do so in any country." On August 7, he and his associates put this manifesto into effect with devastating truck bombings of the US embassies in Kenya and Tanzania.

The CIA had already identified bin Laden's family compound in the open desert near Kandahar Airport, a collection of buildings called Tarnak Farm. It's possible that more satellite footage had, by then, been taken of this site than of any other place on earth; one famous picture seems to show bin Laden standing outside one of his wives' homes. The Agency conceived an elaborate plot to kidnap bin Laden from Tarnak Farm with the help of Afghan operatives and spirit him out of the country, but CIA director George Tenet cancelled the project because of the high risk of civilian casualties; he was resented within the Agency for his timidity. Meanwhile, the White House stationed submarines in the northern Arabian Sea with the map coordinates of Tarnak Farm preloaded into their missile guidance systems. They were waiting for hard evidence from the CIA that bin Laden was in residence.

Within days of the East Africa bombings, Clinton signed a top secret Memorandum of Notification authorizing the CIA to use lethal force against bin Laden. On August 20, 1998, he ordered seventy-five cruise missiles, costing $750,000 each, to be fired at the Zawhar Kili camp (about seven miles south of Khost), the site of a major al Qaeda meeting. The attack killed twenty-one Pakistanis, but bin Laden was forewarned, perhaps by Saudi intelligence. Two of the missiles fell short into Pakistan, causing Islamabad to denounce the US action. At the same time, the US fired thirteen cruise missiles into a chemical plant in Khartoum: the CIA claimed that the plant was partly owned by bin Laden and that it was manufacturing nerve gas. They knew none of this was true.

Clinton had publicly confessed to his sexual liaison with Monica Lewinsky on August 17, and many critics around the world conjectured that both attacks were diversionary measures. (The film *Wag the Dog* had just come out, in which a president in the middle of an election campaign is charged with molesting a Girl Scout and makes it seem as if he's gone to war against Albania to distract people's attention.) As a result Clinton became more cautious, and he and his aides began seriously to question the quality of CIA information. The US bombing in May 1999 of the Chinese embassy in Belgrade, allegedly because of faulty intelligence, further discredited the Agency. A year later, Tenet fired one intelligence officer and reprimanded six managers, including a senior official, for their bungling of that incident.

The Clinton administration made two more attempts to get bin Laden. During the winter of 1998–1999, the CIA confirmed that a large party of Persian Gulf dignitaries had flown into the Afghan desert for a falcon-hunting party, and that bin Laden had joined them. The CIA called for an attack on their encampment until Richard Clarke, Clinton's counterterrorism aide, discovered that among the hosts of the gathering was royalty from the United Arab Emirates. Clarke had been instrumental in a 1998 deal to sell eighty F-16 military jets to the UAE, which was also a crucial supplier of oil and gas to America and its allies. The strike was called off.

THE CIA AS A SECRET PRESIDENTIAL ARMY

Throughout the 1990s, the Clinton administration devoted major resources to the development of a long-distance drone aircraft called Predator, invented by the former chief designer for the Israeli air force, who had emigrated to the United States. In its nose was mounted a Sony digital TV camera, similar to the ones used by news helicopters reporting on freeway traffic or on O. J. Simpson's fevered ride through Los Angeles. By the turn of the century, Agency experts had also added a Hellfire anti-tank missile to the Predator and tested it on a mock-up of Tarnak Farm in the Nevada desert. This new weapons system made it possible instantly to kill bin Laden if the camera spotted him. Unfortunately for the CIA, on one of its flights from Uzbekistan over Tarnak Farm the Predator photographed as a target a child's wooden swing. To his credit, Clinton held back on using the Hellfire because of the virtual certainty of killing bystanders, and Tenet, scared of being blamed for another failure, suggested that responsibility for the armed Predator's use be transferred to the Air Force.

When the new Republican administration came into office, it was deeply uninterested in bin Laden and terrorism even though the outgoing national security adviser, Sandy Berger, warned National Security Adviser Condoleezza Rice that it would be George W. Bush's most serious foreign policy problem. On August 6, 2001, the CIA delivered its daily briefing to Bush at his ranch in Crawford, Texas, with the headline "Bin Laden determined to strike in US," but the president seemed not to notice. Slightly more than a month later, Osama bin Laden successfully brought off perhaps the most significant example of asymmetric warfare in the history of international relations.

Coll has written a powerful indictment of the CIA's myopia and incompetence, but he seems to be of two minds. He occasionally indulges in flights of pro-CIA rhetoric, describing it, for example, as a "vast, pulsing, self-perpetuating, highly sensitive network on continuous alert" whose "listening posts were attuned to even the most isolated and dubious evidence of pending attacks" and whose "analysts were continually encouraged to share information as widely as possible among those with appropriate security clearances." This is nonsense: the early-warning functions of the CIA were upstaged decades ago by covert operations.

Coll acknowledges that every president since Truman, once he discovered that he had a totally secret, financially unaccountable, private army at his personal disposal, found its deployment irresistible. But covert operations usually became entangled in hopeless webs of secrecy, and invariably led to more blowback. Richard Clarke argues that "the CIA used its classification rules not only to protect its agents but also to deflect outside scrutiny of its covert operations," and Peter Tomsen, the former US ambassador to the Afghan resistance during the late 1980s, concludes that "America's failed policies in Afghanistan flowed in part from the compartmented, top secret isolation in which the CIA always sought to work." Excessive, bureaucratic secrecy lies at the heart of the Agency's failures.

Given the Agency's clear role in causing the disaster of September 11, 2001, what we need today is not a new intelligence czar but an end to the secrecy behind which the CIA hides and avoids accountability for its actions. To this day, the CIA continues grossly to distort any and all attempts at a constitutional foreign policy. Although Coll doesn't go on to draw the conclusion, I believe the CIA has outlived any Cold War justification it once might have had and should simply be abolished.

6 MIRAGE OF THE GOOD WAR

By Tariq Ali

Rarely has there been such an enthusiastic display of international unity as that which greeted the invasion of Afghanistan in 2001. Support for the war was universal in the chanceries of the West, even before its aims and parameters had been declared. NATO governments rushed to assert themselves "all for one." Blair jetted round the world, proselytizing the "doctrine of the international community" and the opportunities for peace-keeping and nation-building in the Hindu Kush. Putin welcomed the extension of American bases along Russia's southern borders. Every mainstream Western party endorsed the war; every media network—with BBC World and CNN in the lead—became its megaphone. For the German Greens, as for Laura Bush and Cherie Blair, it was a war for the liberation of the women of Afghanistan.[1] For the White House, a fight for civilization. For Iran, the impending defeat of the Wahhabi enemy.

Three years later, as the chaos in Iraq deepened, Afghanistan became the "good war" by comparison. It had been legitimized by the United Nations— even if the resolution was not passed until after the bombs had finished falling—and backed by NATO. If tactical differences had sharpened over Iraq, they could be resolved in Afghanistan. First Zapatero, then Prodi, then

---

1   In fact, the only period in Afghan history where women were granted equal rights and educated was from 1979 to 1989, the decade it was ruled by the PDPA, backed by Soviet troops. Repressive in many ways, on the health and education fronts real progress was achieved, as in Iraq under Saddam. Hence the nostalgia for the past amongst poorer sections of society in both countries.

Rudd, compensated for pulling troops out of Iraq by dispatching them to Kabul.[2] France and Germany could extol their peace-keeping or civilizing roles there. As suicide bombings increased in Baghdad, Afghanistan was now—for American Democrats keen to prove their "security" credentials— the "real front" of the war on terror, supported by every US presidential candidate in the run-up to the 2008 elections, with Senator Obama pressuring the White House to violate Pakistani sovereignty whenever necessary. With varying degrees of firmness, the occupation of Afghanistan was also supported by China, Iran, and Russia; though in the case of the latter, there was always a strong element of schadenfreude. Soviet veterans of the Afghan War were amazed to see their mistakes now being repeated by the United States, in a war even more inhumane than its predecessor.

Meanwhile, the number of Afghan civilians killed has exceeded many tens of times over the 2,746 who died in Manhattan. Unemployment is around 60 percent, and maternal, infant, and child mortality levels are now among the highest in the world. Opium harvests have soared, and the "Neo-Taliban" is growing stronger year by year. By common consent, Hamid Karzai's government does not even control its own capital, let alone provide an example of "good governance." Reconstruction funds vanish into cronies' pockets or go to pay short-contract Western consultants. Police are predators rather than protectors. The social crisis is deepening. Increasingly, Western commentators have evoked the spectre of failure— usually in order to spur *encore un effort*. A *Guardian* leader summarizes: "Defeat looks possible, with all the terrible consequences that will bring."[3]

---

2   Visiting Madrid after Zapatero's election triumph of March 2008, I was informed by a senior government official that they had considered a total withdrawal from Afghanistan a few months before the polls but had been outmaneuvered by the US promising Spain that the head of its military would be proposed for commander of the NATO forces, and a withdrawal from Kabul would disrupt this possibility. Spain drew back, only to discover it had been tricked.

3   "Failing State," *Guardian*, February 1, 2008; see also "The Good War, Still to Be Won," August 20, 2007; "Gates, Truth and Afghanistan," *New York Times*, February 12, 2008; "Must they be wars without end?" *Economist*, December 13, 2007; International Crisis Group, "Combating Afghanistan's Insurgency," November 2, 2006.

Two principal arguments, often overlapping, are put forward as to "what went wrong" in Afghanistan. For liberal imperialists, the answer can be summarized in two words: "not enough." The invasion organized by Bush, Cheney, and Rumsfeld was done on the cheap. The "light footprint" demanded by the Pentagon meant that there were too few troops on the ground in 2001–2002. Financial commitment to "state-building" was insufficient. Though it may now be too late, the answer is to pour in more troops, more money—"multiple billions" over "multiple years," according to the US Ambassador in Kabul.[4] The second answer—advanced by Karzai and the White House, but propagated by the Western media generally—can be summed up in one word: Pakistan. Neither of these arguments holds water.

POLITICAL FAILURES

True, there was a sense of relief in Kabul when the Taliban's Wahhabite Emirate was overthrown. Though rape and heroin production had been curtailed under their rule, warlords kept at bay and order largely restored in a country that had been racked by foreign and civil wars since 1979, the end result had been a ruthless social dictatorship with a level of control over the everyday lives of ordinary people that made the clerical regime in Iran appear an island of enlightenment. The Taliban government fell without a serious struggle. Islamabad, officially committed to the US cause, forbade any frontal confrontation.[5] Some Taliban zealots crossed the border into Pakistan, while a more independent faction loyal to Mullah Omar decamped to the mountains to fight another day. Kabul was undefended; the BBC war correspondent entered the capital before the Northern Alliance. What many Afghans now expected from a successor government was a similar level of order, minus the repression and social restrictions, and a freeing of the country's spirit. What they were instead presented with was a melancholy spectacle that blasted all their hopes.

The problem was not lack of funds but the Western state-building project

---

4   "CIA Review Highlights Afghan Leader's Woes," *New York Times*, November 5, 2006.

5   Pakistan's key role in securing this "victory" was underplayed in the Western media at the time. The public was told that it was elite Special Forces units and CIA "specialists" that had liberated Afghanistan; having triumphed here they could now be sent on to Iraq.

itself, by its nature an exogenous process—aiming to construct an army able to suppress its own population but incapable of defending the nation from outside powers; a civil administration with no control over planning or social infrastructure, which are in the hands of Western NGOs; and a government whose foreign policy marches in step with Washington's. It bore no relation to the realities on the ground. After the fall of the Taliban government, four major armed groups re-emerged as strong regional players. In the gas-rich and more industrialized north, bordering the Central Asian republics of Uzbekistan and Tajikistan, the Uzbek warlord Rashid Dostum was in charge with his capital in Mazar-i-Sharif. Allied first to the communists, later the Taliban, and most recently NATO, General Dostum had demonstrated his latest loyalty by massacring two to three thousand Taliban and Arab prisoners under the approving gaze of US intelligence personnel in December 2001.

Not too far from Dostum, in the mountainous north-east of the country, a region rich in emeralds, lapis lazuli, and opium, the late Ahmed Shah Massoud had built a fighting organization of Tajiks, who regularly ambushed troops on the Salang Highway that linked Kabul to Tashkent during the Soviet occupation. Massoud had been the leader of the armed wing of Burhanuddin Rabbani's Jamaat-i-Islami, which operated in tandem with an allied Islamist leader, Abd al-Rabb Sayyaf (both men were lecturers in Sharia law at the law faculty of Kabul University in 1973, where these movements were incubated). Until 1993 they were funded by Saudi Arabia, after which the latter gradually shifted its support to the Taliban. Massoud maintained a semi-independence during the Taliban period, up to his death on September 9, 2001.[6] Massoud's supporters are currently in the government, but are not considered one hundred percent reliable as far as NATO is concerned.

To the west, sheltered by neighboring Iran, lies the ancient city of Herat, once a center of learning and culture where poets, artists, and scholars flourished. Among the important works illustrated here over the course of three centuries

---

6   Massoud had been a favorite pin-up in Paris during the Soviet–Afghan war, usually portrayed as a ruggedly romantic, anti-communist Che Guevara. His membership of Rabbani's Islamist group and reactionary views on most social issues were barely mentioned. But if he had presented an image of incorruptible masculinity to his supporters in the West, it was not the same at home. Rape and the heroin trade were not uncommon in areas under his control.

was a fifteenth-century version of the classic *Miraj-nameh*, an early medieval account of the Prophet's ascent to heaven from the Dome of the Rock and the punishments he observed as he passed through hell.[7] In modern Herat, the Shia warlord Ismail Khan holds sway. A former army captain inspired by the Islamic Revolution in Iran, Ismail achieved instant fame by leading a garrison revolt against the pro-Moscow regime in 1979. Backed by Tehran he built up a strong force that united all the Shia groups and were to trouble the Russians throughout their stay. Tens of thousands of refugees from this region (where a Persian dialect is the spoken language) were given work, shelter, and training in Iran. From 1992 to 1995, the province was run on authoritarian lines. It was a harsh regime: Ismail Khan's half-witted effrontery soon began to alienate his allies, while his high-tax and forced conscription policies angered peasant families. By the time the Taliban took power in Kabul in 1996, support had already drained away from the warlord. Herat fell without a struggle, and Ismail was imprisoned by the Taliban, only escaping in March 2000. His supporters meanwhile crossed the border to Iran where they bided their time, to return in October 2001 under NATO cover.

The south was another story again. The Pashtun villages bore the brunt of the fighting during the 1980s and 90s.[8] Rapid population growth, coupled with

---

7   The stunning illustrations were exquisitely calligraphed by Malik Bakshi in the Uighur script. There are sixty-one paintings in all, created with great love for the Prophet of Islam. He is depicted with Central Asian features and seen flying to heaven on a magical steed with a woman's head. There are also illustrations of a meeting with Gabriel and Adam, a sighting of houris at the gates of Paradise, and of winebibbers being punished in hell. European scholars have suggested that an early Latin translation of the poem may have been a source of inspiration for Dante.

8   Afghanistan's ethnography has generated a highly politicized statistical debate. The six-year survey carried out by a Norwegian foundation is probably the most accurate. This suggests that Pashtuns make up an estimated 63 percent of the population, along with the mainly Persian-speaking Tajiks (12 percent), Uzbeks (9 percent), and the mainly Shia Hazaras (6 percent): WAK Foundation, Norway, 1999. The CIA Factbook, by contrast, gives 42, 27, 9, and 9 percent respectively. The tiny non-Muslim minority of Hindus and Sikhs, mainly shopkeepers and traders in Kabul, were displaced by the Taliban; some were killed, and thousands fled to India.

the disruptions of war and the resulting loss of livestock, hastened the collapse of the subsistence economy. In many districts this was replaced by poppy cultivation and the rule of local bandits and strongmen. By the early 1990s, three militant Sunni groups had acquired dominance in the region: the Taliban, the group led by Ahmed Shah Massoud from the Panjshir Province, and the followers of Gulbuddin Hekmatyar, once Pakistan's favorite, who had been groomed by the Saudis as the new leader. The jihad was long over, and now the jihadis were at each other's throats, with control of the drug trade the major stake in a brutal power struggle. Under Benazir Bhutto's second premiership, Pakistan's military backing for the Taliban proved decisive. But the overthrow of the Mullah Omar government in the winter of 2001 saw the re-emergence of many of the local gangsters whose predations it had partly checked.

ANOINTMENT OF KARZAI

Washington assigned the task of assembling a new government to Zalmay Khalilzad, its Afghan-American pro-consul in Kabul. The capital was occupied by competing militias, united only by opposition to the toppled Taliban, and their representatives had to be accommodated on every level. The Northern Alliance candidate for president, Abdul Haq of Jalalabad, had conveniently been captured and executed in October 2001 by the Taliban when he entered the country with a small group from Pakistan. (His supporters alleged betrayal by the CIA and the ISI, who were unhappy about his links to Russia and Iran, and tipped off Mullah Omar.) Another obvious anti-Taliban candidate was Ahmed Shah Massoud; but he had also been killed—by a suicide bomber of unknown provenance—two days before 9/11. Massoud would no doubt have been the EU choice for Afghan president, had he lived; the French government issued a postage stamp with his portrait, and Kabul airport bears his name. Whether he would have proved as reliable a client as Khalilzad's transplanted protégé, Hamid Karzai, must now remain an open question.

Aware that the US could not run the country without the Northern Alliance and its backers in Tehran and Moscow, Khalilzad toned down the emancipatory rhetoric and concentrated on the serious business of occupation. The coalition he constructed resembled a blind octopus, with mainly Tajik limbs and Karzai as its unseeing eye. The Afghan president comes from the Durrani tribe of Pashtuns from Kandahar. His father had served in a junior capacity in Zahir Shah's government. Young Karzai backed the mujahideen against

Russia and later supported the Taliban, though he turned down their offer to become Afghanistan's ambassador to the UN, preferring to relocate and work for the oil company UNOCAL. Here he backed up Khalilzad, who was then representing CentGas in their bid to construct a pipeline that would take gas from Turkmenistan across Afghanistan to Pakistan and India.[9]

After his appointment as interim president, the Saudi daily *Al-Watan* published a revealing profile of Karzai, stating that he had been a CIA pawn since the 1980s, with his status on the Afghan chessboard enhanced every few years:

> Since then, Karzai's ties with the Americans have not been interrupted. At the same time, he established ties with the British and other European and international sides, especially after he became deputy foreign minister in 1992 in the wake of the Afghan mujahideen's assumption of power and the overthrow of the pro-Moscow Najibullah regime. Karzai found no contradiction between his ties with the Americans and his support for the Taliban movement as of 1994, when the Americans had—secretly and through the Pakistanis—supported the Taliban's assumption of power to put an end to the civil war and the actual partition of Afghanistan due to the failure of Burhanuddin Rabbani's experience in ruling the country.[10]

---

9 The CentGas consortium, incorporated in 1997, included UNOCAL, Gazprom, Hyundai, and oil companies from Saudi Arabia, Japan, and Pakistan. In late 1997 a Taliban delegation received full honors when they visited UNOCAL headquarters, hoping to sign the $3.5 billion pipeline contract. According to the *Sunday Telegraph* ("Oil Barons Court Taliban in Texas," December 14, 1997): "the Islamic warriors appear to have been persuaded to close the deal, not through delicate negotiation but by old-fashioned Texan hospitality. Dressed in traditional *shalwar kameez,* Afghan waistcoats and loose, black turbans, the high-ranking delegation was given VIP treatment during the four-day stay." The project was suspended in 1998, as the Taliban were split on whom to award the pipeline project to: Mullah Rabbani preferred the offer from the Argentine company Bridas, while Mullah Omar was strongly in favor of the American-led deal. But US–Taliban contacts continued till mid-2001 both in Islamabad and New York, where the Taliban maintained a "diplomatic office" headed by Abdul Hakim Mojahed.

10 BBC Monitoring Service, December 15, 2001.

Karzai was duly installed in December 2001, but intimacy with US intelligence networks failed to translate into authority or legitimacy at home. Karzai harbored no illusions about his popularity in the country. He knew his biological and political life was heavily dependent on the occupation, and demanded a bodyguard of US Marines or American mercenaries, rather than a security detail from his own ethnic Pashtun base.[11] There were at least three coup attempts against him in 2002–2003 by his Northern Alliance allies; these were fought off by the ISAF, which was largely tied down in assuring Karzai's security—while also providing a vivid illustration of where his support lay.[12] A quick-fix presidential contest organized at great expense by Western PR firms in October 2004—just in time for the US elections—failed to bolster support for the puppet president inside the country. Karzai's habit of parachuting his relatives and protégés into provincial governor or police chief jobs has driven many local communities into alliance with the Taliban, as the main anti-government force. In Zabul, Helmand and elsewhere, all the insurgents had to do was "approach the victims of the pro-Karzai strongmen and promise them protection and support. Attempts by local elders to seek protection in Kabul routinely ended nowhere, as the wrongdoers enjoyed either direct US support or Karzai's sympathy."[13]

Nor is it any secret that Karzai's younger brother, Ahmed Wali Karzai, has now become one of the richest drug barons in the country. At a meeting with Pakistan's president in 2005, when Karzai was bleating about Pakistan's inability to stop cross-border smuggling, Musharraf suggested that perhaps Karzai should set an example by bringing his sibling under control. (The hatred for each other of these two close allies of Washington is well known in the region.)

NEW INEQUALITIES

Also feeding the resentment is the behavior of a new elite clustered

---

11   The late Benazir Bhutto made the same request for American protection on her return to Pakistan, but in her case it was vetoed by Islamabad.

12   Barry McCaffrey, "Trip to Afghanistan and Pakistan," US Military Academy Memorandum, West Point, New York, 2006, 8.

13   Antonio Giustozzi, *Koran, Kalashnikov and Laptop: the Neo-Taliban Insurgency in Afghanistan*, New York: Columbia University Press, 2007, 60. The corruption and brutality of the newly established Afghan National Police is also widely credited with turning the population against the Karzai government.

around Karzai and the occupying forces, which has specialized in creaming off foreign aid to create its own criminal networks of graft and patronage. The corruptions of this layer grow each month like an untreated tumor. Western funds are siphoned off to build fancy homes for the native enforcers. Housing scandals erupted as early as 2002, when cabinet ministers awarded themselves and favored cronies prime real estate in Kabul where land prices were rocketing, since the occupiers and their camp followers had to live in the style to which they were accustomed. Karzai's colleagues, protected by ISAF troops, built their large villas in full view of the mud-brick hovels of the poor. The burgeoning slum settlements of Kabul, where the population has now swollen to an estimated three million, are a measure of the social crisis that has engulfed the country.

The ancient city has suffered cruelly over the past thirty years. Jade Maiwand, the modernized "Oxford Street" cut through the center in the 1970s, was reduced to rubble during the warfare of 1992–1996. An American-Afghan architect describes how Kabul has been relentlessly transformed

> from a modern capital, to the military and political headquarters of an invading army, to the besieged seat of power of a puppet regime, to the front lines of factional conflict resulting in the destruction of two-thirds of its urban mass, to the testing fields of religious fanaticism which erased from the city the final layers of urban life, to the target of an international war on terrorism.[14]

Yet never have such gaping inequalities featured on this scale before. Little of the supposed $19 billion "aid and reconstruction" money has reached the majority of Afghans. The mains electricity supply is worse now than five years ago, and while the rich can use private generators to power their air conditioners, hot-water heaters, computers, and satellite TVs, average Kabulis "suffered a summer without fans and face a winter without heaters."[15] As a result, hundreds of shelterless Afghans are literally freezing to death each winter.

Then there are the NGOs who descended on the country like locusts after the occupation. As one observer reported: "A reputed 10,000 NGO staff have

14   Ajmal Maiwandi, "Re-Doing Kabul," presented at the London School of Economics, July 11, 2002.
15   Barnett Rubin, "Saving Afghanistan," *Foreign Affairs*, January–February 2007.

turned Kabul into the Klondike during the gold rush, building office blocks, driving up rents, cruising about in armoured jeeps and spending stupefying sums of other people's money, essentially on themselves. They take orders only from some distant agency, but then the same goes for the American army, NATO, the UN, the EU and the supposedly sovereign Afghan government."[16]

Even supporters of the occupation have lost patience with these bodies, and some of the most successful candidates in the 2005 National Assembly elections made an attack on them a centerpiece of their campaigns. Worse, according to one US specialist, "their well-funded activities highlighted the poverty and ineffectiveness of the civil administration and discredited its local representatives in the eyes of the local populace."[17] Unsurprisingly, NGO employees began to be targeted by the insurgents, including in the north, and had to hire mercenary protection.

In sum: even in the estimate of the West's own specialists and institutions, "nation-building" in Afghanistan has been flawed in its very conception. It has so far produced a puppet president dependent for his survival on foreign mercenaries, a corrupt and abusive police force, a "nonfunctioning" judiciary, a thriving criminal layer, and a deepening social and economic crisis. It beggars belief to argue that "more of this" will be the answer to Afghanistan's problems.

AN AFGHAN SURGE?

The argument that more NATO troops are the solution is equally unsustainable. All the evidence suggests that the brutality of the occupying forces has been one of the main sources of recruits for the Taliban. American air power, lovingly referred to as "Big Daddy" by frightened US soldiers on unwelcoming terrain, is far from paternal when it comes to targeting Pashtun villages. There is widespread fury among Afghans at the number of civilian casualties, many of them children. There have been numerous incidents of rape and rough treatment of women by ISAF soldiers, as well as indiscriminate

---

16   Simon Jenkins, "It Takes Inane Optimism to See Victory in Afghanistan," *Guardian*, August 8, 2007.
17   S. Frederick Starr, "Sovereignty and Legitimacy in Afghan Nation-Building," in Fukuyama, ed., *Nation-Building Beyond Afghanistan and Iraq*, Baltimore: Johns Hopkins University Press, 2006, 117.

bombing of villages and house-to-house search-and-arrest missions. The behavior of the foreign mercenaries backing up the NATO forces is just as bad. Even sympathetic observers admit that "their alcohol consumption and patronage of a growing number of brothels in Kabul . . . is arousing public anger and resentment."[18] To this could be added the deaths by torture at the US-run Bagram prison and the resuscitation of a Soviet-era security law under which detainees are being sentenced to twenty-year jail terms on the basis of summary allegations by US military authorities. All this creates a thirst for dignity that can only be assuaged by genuine independence.

Talk of "victory" sounds increasingly hollow to Afghan ears. Many who detest the Taliban are so angered by the failures of NATO and the behavior of its troops that they are pleased there is some opposition. What was initially viewed by some locals as a necessary police action against al Qaeda following the 9/11 attacks is now perceived by a growing majority in the region as a fully fledged imperial occupation. Successive recent reports have suggested that the unpopularity of the government and the "disrespectful" behavior of the occupying troops have had the effect of creating nostalgia for the time when the Taliban were in power. The repression leaves people with no option but to back those trying to resist, especially in a part of the world where the culture of revenge is strong. When a whole community feels threatened it reinforces solidarity, regardless of the character or weakness of those who fight back. This does not just apply to the countryside. The mass protests in Kabul, when civilians were killed by an American military vehicle, signaled the obvious targets:

Rioters chanted slogans against the United States and President Karzai and attacked the Parliament building, the offices of media outlets and nongovernmental organizations, diplomatic residences, brothels, and hotels and restaurants that purportedly served alcohol. The police, many of whom disappeared, proved incompetent, and the vulnerability of the government to mass violence became clear.[19]

---

18   Barnett Rubin, "Proposals for Improved Stability in Afghanistan," in Ivo Daalder, et al., eds, *Crescent of Crisis: US–European Strategy for the Greater Middle East*, Washington, DC: The Brookings Institute, 2006, 149.
19   Rubin, "Saving Afghanistan."

As the British and Russians discovered to their cost in the preceding two centuries, Afghans do not like being occupied. If a second-generation Taliban is now growing and creating new alliances it is not because its sectarian religious practices have become popular, but because it is the only available umbrella for national liberation. Initially, the middle-cadre Taliban who fled across the border in November 2001 and started low-level guerrilla activity the following year attracted only a trickle of new recruits from madrasas and refugee camps. From 2004 onwards, increasing numbers of young Waziris were radicalized by Pakistani military and police incursions in the tribal areas, as well as devastating attacks on villages by unmanned US "drones." At the same time, the movement was starting to win active support from village mullahs in Zabul, Helmand, Ghazni, Paktika, and Kandahar provinces, and then in the towns. By 2006 there were reports of Kabul mullahs who had previously supported Karzai's allies but were now railing against the foreigners and the government; calls for jihad against the occupiers were heard in the north-east border provinces of Takhar and Badakhshan.

The largest pool for new Taliban recruits, according to a well-informed recent estimate, has been "communities antagonized by the local authorities and security forces." In Kandahar, Helmand, and Uruzgan, Karzai's cronies—district and provincial governors, security bosses, police chiefs—are quite prepared to tip off US troops against their local rivals, as well as subjecting the latter to harassment and extortion. In these circumstances, the Taliban are the only available defense. (According to the same report, the Taliban themselves have claimed that families driven into refugee camps by indiscriminate US airpower attacks on their villages have been their major source of recruits.) By 2006 the movement was winning the support of traders and businessmen in Kandahar, and led a mini "Tet offensive" there that year. One reason suggested for their increasing support in towns is that the new-model Taliban have relaxed their religious strictures, for males at least—no longer demanding beards or banning music—and improved their propaganda, producing cassette tapes and CDs of popular singers, and DVDs of US and Israeli atrocities in Iraq, Lebanon, and Palestine.[20]

The re-emergence of the Taliban cannot therefore simply be blamed on Islamabad's failure to police the border, or cut "command and control" links,

---

20   Giustozzi, *Koran, Kalashnikov and Laptop*, 42, 69.

as the Americans claim. While the ISI played a crucial role in bringing the Taliban to power in 1996 and in the retreat of 2001, they no longer have the same degree of control over a more diffuse and widespread movement, for which the occupation itself has been the main recruiting sergeant. It is a traditional colonial ploy to blame "outsiders" for internal problems: Karzai specializes in this approach. If anything, the destabilization functions in the other direction: the war in Afghanistan has created a critical situation in two Pakistani frontier provinces, and the use of the Pakistan army by Centcom has resulted in suicide terrorism in Lahore, where the Federal Investigation Agency and the Naval War College have been targeted by supporters of the Afghan insurgents. The Pashtun majority in Afghanistan has always had close links to its fellow Pashtuns in Pakistan. The present border was an imposition by the British Empire, but it has always remained porous. It is virtually impossible to build a Texan-style fence or an Israeli wall across the mountainous and largely unmarked 1,500-mile frontier that separates the two countries.

OLDER MODELS

The current occupation of Afghanistan naturally recalls colonial operations in the region, not just to Afghans but to some Western myth-makers— usually British, but with a few Subcontinental mimics—who try to draw lessons from the older model; the implication being that the British were "good imperialists" who have a great deal to teach the brutish, impatient Americans. The British administrators were, for the most part, racist to the core, and their self-proclaimed "competence" involved the efficient imposition of social apartheid in every colony they controlled. They could be equally brutal in Africa, the Middle East, and India. Though a promise of civilizational uplift was required as ideological justification, then as now, the facts of the colonial legacy speak for themselves. In 1947, the year the British left India, the overwhelming majority of midnight's children were illiterate, and 85 percent of the economy was rural.[21]

---

21 "Per capita income was about one-twentieth of the level then attained in developed countries ... Illiteracy was a high 84 per cent and the majority (60 per cent) of children in the six to eleven age-group did not attend school; mass communicable diseases (malaria, smallpox and cholera) were widespread and, in the absence of a good public health service and sanitation, mortality rates (27

Not bad intentions or botched initiatives, but the imperial presence itself was the problem. Kipling is much quoted today by editorialists urging a bigger Western "footprint" in Afghanistan, but even he was fully aware of the hatred felt by the Pashtuns for the British, and wrote as much in one of his last dispatches from Peshawar in April 1885 to the *Civil and Military Gazette* in Lahore:

> Pathans, Afridis, Logas, Kohistanis, Turcomans and a hundred other varieties of the turbulent Afghan race, are gathered in the vast human menagerie between the Edwardes Gate and the Ghor Khutri. As an Englishman passes, they will turn to scowl on him, and in many cases to spit fluently on the ground after he has passed. One burly, big-paunched ruffian, with shaven head and a neck creased and dimpled with rolls of fat, is specially zealous in this religious rite—contenting himself with no perfunctory performance, but with a whole-souled expectoration, that must be as refreshing to his comrades as it is disgusting to the European.

One reason among many for the Pashtuns' historic resentment was the torching of the famous bazaar in Kabul, a triumph of Mughal architecture. Ali Mardan Khan, a renowned governor, architect and engineer, had built the *chahr-chatta* (four-sided) roofed and arcaded central market in the seventeenth century on the model of those in old Euro-Arabian Muslim cities—Cairo, Damascus, Baghdad, Palermo or Córdoba. It was regarded as unique in the region; nothing on the same scale was built in Lahore or Delhi. The bazaar was deliberately destroyed in 1842 by General Pollock's "Army of Retribution," remembered as amongst the worst killers, looters and marauders ever to arrive in Afghanistan, a contest in which competition remains strong. Defeated in a number of cities and forced to evacuate Kabul, the British punished its citizens by removing the market from the map. What will remain of Kabul when the current occupiers finally withdraw has yet to be seen, but its spreading mass of deeply impoverished squatter settlements suggest that it is set to be one of the major new capitals of the "planet of slums."[22]

---

per 1,000) were very high." Dharma Kumar and Meghnad Desai, eds, *Cambridge Economic History of India*, vol. II: *c.1757–c.1970*, Cambridge: Cambridge University Press, 1983, 23.

22   Mike Davis, "Planet of Slums," *NLR* 26, March–April 2004, 13.

The Western occupation of Afghanistan is now confronted with five seemingly intractable, interrelated problems. The systemic failures of its nation-building strategy, the corruption of its local agents, the growing alienation of large sectors of the population and the strengthening of armed resistance are all compounded by the distortions wrought by the opium-heroin industry on the country's economy. According to UN estimates, narcotics account for 53 percent of the country's gross domestic product, and the poppy fields continue to spread. Some 90 percent of the world opium supply emanates from Afghanistan. Since 2003 the NATO mission has made no serious attempt to bring about a reduction in this lucrative trade. Karzai's own supporters would rapidly desert if their activities in this sphere were disrupted, and the amount of state help needed over many years to boost agriculture and cottage industries and reduce dependence on poppy farming would require an entirely different set of priorities. Only a surreal utopian could expect NATO countries, busy privatizing and deregulating their own economies, to embark upon full-scale national development projects abroad.

NATO'S GOALS

It need hardly be added that the bombardment and occupation of Afghanistan has been a disastrous—and predictable—failure in capturing the perpetrators of 9/11. This could only have been the result of effective police work, not of international war and military occupation. Everything that has happened in Afghanistan since 2001—not to mention Iraq, Palestine, and Lebanon—has had the opposite effect, as the West's own intelligence reports have repeatedly confirmed. According to the official 9/11 Commission report, Mullah Omar's initial response to Washington's demands that Osama bin Laden be handed over and al Qaeda deprived of a safe haven was "not negative"; he himself had opposed any al Qaeda attack on US targets.[23] But while the Mullah was playing for time, the White House closed down negotiations. It required a swift war of revenge. Afghanistan had been denominated the first port of call in the "global war on terror," with Iraq already the Administration's main target. The shock-and-awe six-week aerial onslaught that followed was merely a drumroll for the forthcoming

---

23   *The 9/11 Commission Report*, New York: W. W. Norton & Company, 2004, 333–4, 251–2.

intervention in Iraq, with no military rationale in Afghanistan. Predictably, it only gave al Qaeda leaders the chance to vanish into the hills. To portray the invasion as a "war of self-defense" for NATO makes a mockery of international law, which was perverted to twist a flukishly successful attack by a tiny, terrorist Arab groupuscule into an excuse for an open-ended American military thrust into the Middle East and Central Eurasia.

Herein lie the reasons for the near unanimity among Western opinion-makers that the occupation must not only continue but expand—"many billions over many years." They are to be sought not in the mountain fastnesses of Afghanistan, but in Washington and Brussels. As the *Economist* summarizes, "Defeat would be a body blow not only to the Afghans, but"—and more importantly, of course—"to the NATO alliance."[24] As ever, geopolitics prevails over Afghan interests in the calculus of the big powers. The basing agreement signed by the US with its appointee in Kabul in May 2005 gives the Pentagon the right to maintain a massive military presence in Afghanistan in perpetuity, potentially including nuclear missiles. That Washington is not seeking permanent bases in this fraught and inhospitable terrain simply for the sake of "democratization and good governance" was made clear by NATO's Secretary-General Jaap de Hoop Scheffer at the Brookings Institution in February 2009: a permanent NATO presence in a country that borders the ex-Soviet republics, China, Iran and Pakistan was too good to miss.[25]

More strategically, Afghanistan has become a central theater for reconstituting, and extending, the West's power-political grip on the world order. It provides, first, an opportunity for the US to shrug off problems in persuading its allies to play a broader role in Iraq. As Obama and Clinton have stressed, America and its allies "have greater unity of purpose in Afghanistan. The ultimate outcome of NATO's effort to stabilize Afghanistan and US leadership of that effort may well affect the cohesiveness of the alliance and Washington's ability to shape NATO's future."[26] Beyond this, it is the rise of China that has prompted NATO strategists to propose a vastly

---

24   "Must they be wars without end?"

25   "Afghanistan and NATO: Forging the 21st-Century Alliance," February 29, 2008; transcript available at www.brookings.edu.

26   Paul Gallis, "NATO in Afghanistan," CRS Report for Congress, October 23, 2007.

expanded role for the Western military alliance. Once focused on the Euro-Atlantic area, a recent essay in *NATO Review* suggests, "in the twenty-first century NATO must become an alliance *founded* on the Euro-Atlantic area, designed to project systemic stability beyond its borders":

> The centre of gravity of power on this planet is moving inexorably eastward . . . The Asia-Pacific region brings much that is dynamic and positive to this world, but as yet the rapid change therein is neither stable nor embedded in stable institutions. Until this is achieved, it is the strategic responsibility of Europeans and North Americans, and the institutions they have built, to lead the way . . . security effectiveness in such a world is impossible without both legitimacy and capability.[27]

The only way to protect the international system the West has built, the author continues, is to "re-energize" the transatlantic relationship: "There can be no systemic security without Asian security, and there will be no Asian security without a strong role for the West therein."

These ambitions have yet to be realized. In Afghanistan there were angry street demonstrations against Karzai's signing of the US bases agreement—a clear indication, if one was still needed, that NATO will have to take Karzai with them if they withdraw. Uzbekistan responded by asking the United States to withdraw its base and personnel from their country. The Russians and Chinese are reported to have protested strongly in private, and subsequently conducted joint military operations on each other's territory for the first time: "concern over apparent US plans for permanent bases in Afghanistan and Central Asia" was an important cause of their rapprochement.[28] More limply, Iran responded by increasing export duties, bringing construction in Herat to a halt.[29]

There are at least two routes out of the Khyber impasse. The first and worst

---

27   Julian Lindley-French, "Big World, Big Future, Big NATO," *NATO Review*, Winter 2005.

28   Rubin, "Proposals for Improved Stability in Afghanistan."

29   In response to Karzai's pleas, Tehran proposed a treaty that would prohibit foreign intelligence operations in each country against the other; it is hard to see how Karzai could have signed this with a straight face.

would be to Balkanize the country. This appears to be the dominant pattern of imperial hegemony at the moment, but whereas the Kurds in Iraq and the Kosovars and others in the former Yugoslavia were willing client-nationalists, the likelihood of Tajiks or Hazaras playing this role effectively is more remote in Afghanistan. Some US intelligence officers have been informally discussing the creation of a Pashtun state that unites the tribes and dissolves the Durand Line, but this would destabilize Pakistan and Afghanistan to such a degree that the consequences would be unpredictable. In any event there appear to be no takers in either country at the moment.

The alternative would require a withdrawal of all US forces, either preceded or followed by a regional pact to guarantee Afghan stability for the next ten years. Pakistan, Iran, India, Russia, and, possibly, China could guarantee and support a functioning national government, pledged to preserve the ethnic and religious diversity of Afghanistan and create a space in which all its citizens can breathe, think, and eat every day. It would need a serious social and economic plan to rebuild the country and provide the basic necessities for its people. This would not only be in the interests of Afghanistan, it would be seen as such by its people—physically, politically, and morally exhausted by decades of war and two occupations. Violence, arbitrary or deliberate, has been their fate for too long. They want the nightmare to end and not be replaced with horrors of a different kind. Religious extremists would get short shrift from the people if they disrupted an agreed peace and began a jihad to recreate the Taliban Emirate of Mullah Omar.

The US occupation has not made this task easy. Its predictable failures have revived the Taliban, and increasingly the Pashtuns are uniting behind them. But though the Taliban have been entirely conflated with al Qaeda in the Western media, most of their supporters are driven by local concerns; their political evolution would be more likely to parallel that of Pakistan's domesticated Islamists if the invaders were to leave. A NATO withdrawal could facilitate a serious peace process. It might also benefit Pakistan, provided its military leaders abandoned foolish notions of "strategic depth" and viewed India not as an enemy but as a possible partner in creating a cohesive regional framework within which many contentious issues could be resolved. Are Pakistan's military leaders and politicians capable of grasping the nettle and moving their country forward? Will Washington let them? The solution is political, not military. And it lies in the region, not in Washington or Brussels.

7 CHAOS CENTRAL

By Chris Sands

As the summer of 2005 began its slow fade into autumn, a piece of newspaper wrapped around a kebab said Osama bin Laden had moved to Iraq. It seemed everyone had forgotten there was a war on here. American soldiers used those remaining days of sunshine to buy carpets in Kabul's Chicken Street bazaar, not caring when they were charged over the odds. Elsewhere, mercenaries downed cheap Russian vodka in phoney restaurants before wandering up a few stairs to sleep with Chinese prostitutes whose pimps bribed local government officials. The brothels were often in the same neighborhoods as the mansions that militia commanders were building themselves with CIA funds and drug money.

Back then, this beautiful city was the ideal place for a bit of post-conflict profiteering. Hastily created NGOs continued to flood in, eager for a slice of the action. So did journalists determined to write about democracy, the suave English-speaking president, and the local golf course. It was the calm before the storm. Victory had been declared, and, while Afghans were starting to feel the weight of its baggage, the rest of the world was still having fun at their expense.

But the decadence and ignorance were never going to be allowed to last for long, and the Taliban knew their time was coming again. The warning signs were around for anyone who cared to look.

I'd been in Afghanistan less than a week when aid groups revealed that deteriorating security had put their projects under threat. They feared they had become targets for the insurgency. A little while afterwards, the governor of Maidan Wardak, a province bordering Kabul, told me all was okay there. Then the PR finished and he cut loose. A new generation of militants had shown its face, he said. They were young men disillusioned with the occupation, and some were trained in Pakistan. Trouble was also evident near the eastern city of Jalalabad, where a villager complained that his cousin had vanished since being arrested by the Americans roughly three years earlier. We talked in a dirt yard full of kids, and I think they were the only ones who expected his return.

The south, though, was where the pieces of the jigsaw began to fit together. Kandahar is the spiritual heartland of the Taliban, and in late 2005 the movement was again drawing strength from its birthplace. There, for the first time, I caught sight of a reality our politicians had made us believe did not exist.

A man working at the football stadium reminisced fondly about the old days when executions happened on the pitch. If capital punishment was still common, he said, the new government wouldn't be so crooked. This was something I would hear repeatedly, until eventually it was said by Afghans across the country. The police were the worst offenders, looking for bribes at every opportunity, to supplement their low wages. Another Kandahari had joined the Taliban as a teenager in the 1990s. "At that time we were very happy," he said. "It was like we were very poor and had suddenly found a lot of money." Talibs are good people and they can never be beaten, he continued. Now they have no choice but to fight because otherwise the Americans will send them to Guantanamo Bay. Most importantly for the future, he revealed that a number of local religious clerics had just declared a jihad.

Insurgent attacks and violent crime were already a problem in Kandahar by then. It was like "living under a knife," said a fifty-three-year-old in the city. Yet even as civilians died, the Taliban were rarely the subject of people's fury. Directly or indirectly, they blamed the government and its allies.

TALIBAN ON THE RISE

In the spring of 2006 Kabul's imams decided to speak out against all this and more. Officials were lining their own pockets, and alcohol was easily available, they said. They were also angry at the house raids conducted by foreign soldiers in rural areas, and accused them of molesting women during the searches. Most said the time for jihad was approaching, and one announced that armed resistance was now the answer.

So when rioters tore through the capital on May 29, it was no big surprise. The spark for that particular day of unrest was a fatal traffic accident involving US troops, but the explosion had been primed long before. Protesters shouted "Death to America," and by the end of the anarchy at least seventeen people had lost their lives. The situation was now ripe for the Taliban to harness national discontent and kick-start a major revolt, and this is exactly what they did.

When British troops had first arrived in Helmand that February, they had come ostensibly to allow reconstruction. The then defense minister John Reid said he would be "perfectly happy" if they did not have to fire a single shot. Instead, they soon found themselves bogged down in some of their worst fighting since the World War II, at times being drawn into hand-to-hand combat. Over 100 have died in the ensuing years.

The Taliban's remit also grew stronger in areas close to Kabul, and two hours from the capital people were warning that the government might collapse. I couldn't find anyone in Ghazni who admitted to taking the insurgents' side: they usually said poverty and a lack of reconstruction were causing people to rebel. Looking at the broken roads and crumbling homes, it wasn't hard to understand what they meant.

Not long before, police in one of the province's districts had tried to stop the Taliban's favorite mode of transport by banning the use of motorbikes. The militants responded by imposing travel restrictions on the whole of that area's population. At night they would go to mosques and tell worshippers not to drive to the provincial capital. "They say 'if you don't cooperate with us we will kill you,'" was how one man described their tactics. "What would be the natural human response to that? Of course you will cooperate."

AN EMERGING PATTERN

A pattern was emerging. The more the Taliban turned to violence, the more they came to be regarded as an omnipresent force that could not be stopped. The bloodshed made people long for the stability of the old regime, if not its repressive laws. Villagers across the south and east had gained almost nothing from the US-led invasion and, in fact, many had lost the little they previously had: good security. Among people in Logar, another of those sad provinces bordering Kabul, the anger was palpable. "Our biggest problem is with the foreigners—we just hate them. Our families, our children, our women—everyone hates them," said an elder. "Let's pretend I'm a young man," said someone else. "I have graduated from school but I can't go to university and there is no factory to work in. So how can I feed myself? I can just join the insurgents—it's easy."

The Taliban first rose up in 1994, when Afghanistan was controlled by warlords still high from the CIA support they had been receiving a few years earlier. A similar thing was happening again, and the movement's original members were quick to see that.

Mullah Wakil Ahmad Mutawakil lost his father during the Soviet occupation and joined the Taliban, he said, "to give the country freedom." He went on to become Mullah Omar's spokesman and later his foreign minister. We talked on a freezing January morning in 2007 when Mutawakil was being kept under watch in Kabul. He knew his government had made mistakes, particularly in letting jihadis from across the world train and fight here. But he was adamant that the international community's decision to isolate the regime had only made it more extreme. "The interesting thing from that time, and lots of people are remembering this now, is the tight security," he said.

Kandahar was frightening that spring of 2007. The police were accused of carrying out kidnappings and robberies, and the scars of suicide bombings pockmarked the streets. There was a lot of anger, despair, and black humor around. Residents expressed a grudging admiration for the old ways of the Taliban simply because the alternatives had come to appear so dire. To them, democracy meant virtual anarchy and, in the villages, a brutal occupation. "If I sit at a table with an American and he says he has brought us freedom, I will tell him he has fucked us," said a father of two. He had fled Kandahar during the Taliban government because he was against its restrictions on education. "But I was never worried about my family," he added. "Every single minute of the last three years I have been very worried."

Comments like this came thick and fast, mixed in with jokes. Some of the men insulted the president, Hamid Karzai, and his wife, laughing and swearing as they did so. A woman I met was sure the city had been better under the Taliban. "If we did not have a full stomach we could at least get some food and go to sleep," she said.

SLIPPING INTO CHAOS

On and on it went, a litany of complaints and stories that portrayed a nation slipping deep into chaos. A religious leader from the district of Panjwayi described how eighteen of his relatives had been killed in an air strike. Then three Talibs from Helmand defended the insurgency as being a natural reaction to events. Basically, they felt they had nothing to lose.

Reports of civilians getting bombed from above came regular as clockwork that spring and summer. First some villagers or local officials would say innocent people were dead, and the NATO or US-led coalition would deny it. Then all parties would agree civilian blood had been spilt, but argue over casualty figures. Hamid Karzai kept demanding that the carnage stop, but it never did.

In Kabul, a senator from Helmand said it was killing the entire country. He was among members of parliament's upper chamber who had called for a ceasefire and negotiations with insurgent groups. They had also said a date should be set for the withdrawal of foreign forces. By then the parliament, supposedly the shining light of a new democracy, was actually a symbol of the Taliban's resurgence. Police in riot gear stood watch, and the building was falling to pieces, with paint flaking away and the walls starting to crack. Not only was there sympathy for the militants inside, there were also men whose viciousness had caused the movement to form in the first place. Most Afghans wanted the warlords brought to justice, but instead the international community had let them stand for election, and here they were showing off their power yet again.

Mullah Abdul Salam Zaeef knew the impact that was having. He used to serve as the Taliban's ambassador to Pakistan, and, after initially being sent to Guantanamo, he was another of the old guard now living under constant surveillance in Kabul. He refused to talk about his stint in US custody, but he was quick to highlight that men with blood on their hands were now the West's great hope. "At the time of the Taliban if someone killed another person it was possible to capture him, send him to court, punish him and execute him. Today, if someone goes to a village and kills 100 people, tomorrow he is given more privileges by the government," he told me. "The Americans and the world community brought the warlords to power. They are supporting them for their benefit against the Taliban, but they know these people are not liked."

By summer 2007 the horror could not be ignored, even in Kabul. Suicide bombings were the main weapon of choice, and they struck fear into Afghans like nothing else, having been unheard-of during the Soviet occupation.

For all their rhetoric about fighting for freedom, justice, and the Almighty, it was also obvious that some in the Taliban were willing to murder anyone to achieve their aim.

This was clear in the pieces of charred flesh and hair that lay scattered in the dust after a bus was blown up near a police headquarters in the city on June 17. And it was evident amidst the smell of shit that filled Pul-e-Charkhi jail, where a prisoner was quick to declare his intentions. "I tell you, when I get out of here the first thing I will do is kill journalists and infidels," he said. "I will kill journalists because they are all spies."

"FOR THIS I BLAME AMERICA"

As 2007 drew to an end, men who hated the Taliban were starting to resemble them. A former Northern Alliance commander from the province of Badakhshan summed it up nicely: "Now when any foreigner is killed every Afghan says 'praise be to God,'" he told me. We were chatting at his home in an area of Kabul where the poor had been forced out so warlords and foreign contractors could move in. He owned a small house and, in front of that, a half-built mansion that he could not afford to finish off. Possibly the only optimists left were the American ambassador and any locals who had the money to take long holidays in Dubai.

Afghanistan's Sikh and Hindu community had been about 50,000 strong before 1992. Now it was down to 5,000. The exodus had been instigated by the mujahideen, not the Taliban. With the same old faces back in power again, no one was happy. "The Taliban told us we had to do all our religious ceremonies in private, but they did not stop us from doing them. It was a government that was not recognized by the world, but it was better than now," said a Sikh.

Even the section of society that should have benefited most from the US-led invasion was full of sorrow. Female MPs told me they felt ashamed for not being able to help their constituents. One said she was sure the time was approaching when she would be a prisoner in her own home again. "For all this I blame America. When the Russians were here the people picked up guns to fight them. Now people are picking up guns to fight the

Americans," she said. "Soon my daughter will finish school, and then she wants to start private education," said another. "But I cannot let her because I cannot give her a bodyguard."

"EVERYTHING IS SCREWED UP"

In January 2008 the streets were a bleak monochrome and the graveyards that dominate Kabul's landscape gave me a glimpse of the future. I interviewed a judge at the Supreme Court who admitted what everyone already knew: certain people here are above the law. He was too scared to name names, but he described the control warlords have over his colleagues as "totally ordinary." Barely had he spoken and the Taliban attacked a luxury hotel in the city. Foreigners were shocked. Afghans just shrugged.

Kandahar was so bad I felt sick before returning there in early spring. Luckily, a friend of mine reassured me that, as a Pashtun, he would offer unconditional protection. "Mullah Omar destroyed Afghanistan because of Osama bin Laden, but he didn't give him up," he said. A day later a Taliban commander from Helmand described how the resistance had struggled to find support in the early years. But after innocent people had been detained or killed the jihad had burst into life. Now even the Afghan army secretly gave them bullets and treated their wounded.

The story of the insurgency, though, no longer required a great deal of traveling. In April I took the short drive from Kabul city to Paghman, and all I found where the offices of Zafar Radio used to be was a pile of burnt trash. Masked men had torched the premises for being "un-Islamic."

In the summer, it got worse. I met an Afghan American who said that "everything is screwed up." Then on July 7, a car bomber attacked the Indian embassy. The huge explosion left corpses scattered around and the wounded dazed and bloodied. By the next morning people were venting their anger at the government, saying it was unable to provide security. When Barack Obama arrived during his presidential campaign, optimism was hard to find. In an area of the capital where Hamid Karzai had narrowly escaped an assassination attempt in the spring, a qualified doctor sold samosas from a roadside stall because it was the only job he could get. "The politics will not change," he said.

2008 was the grimmest year since the invasion. On the seventh anniversary of 9/11, the annual death toll for US troops here had reached new heights: the 113 killed up to September were two more than for the whole of 2007.

Civilians are paying a heavier price. Caught between a rapidly developing insurgency and an occupation force over-reliant on air strikes, they are dropping like flies: according to the UN, 1,445 were killed from January to August 2008 alone.

The Taliban's strength is growing on Kabul's doorstep, in the provinces of Maidan Wardak and Logar. The main highway south is a turkey shoot that no one sensible travels along. In the east of the country, the rebels have taken new ground as they move freely across the border. In the north, warlords are reasserting their dominance—raping and beheading at will. The violence affects us all. Kabul is a claustrophobic, paranoid place. Rockets occasionally land in the streets, ugly concrete barriers have appeared, and Afghans kidnap each other for ransom. Last autumn, on a bright October morning, a British aid worker was murdered in a part of the city regarded as safe.

More foreign troops are due to be sent. But they risk the kind of backlash experienced by the Soviets, and the long-term aim is unclear. After all these years, there are no firm ideas about the way forward. For now the bitter cold has brought the usual lull. But how much more violence will come this spring?

Part II INCOMPETENCE, CORRUPTION, AND THE WAR ON WOMEN

8 MEET THE AFGHAN ARMY: IS IT A FIGMENT OF WASHINGTON'S IMAGINATION?

By Ann Jones

The big Afghanistan debate in Washington is not over whether more troops are needed, but just who they should be: Americans or Afghans—Us or Them. Having just spent time in Afghanistan seeing how things stand, I wouldn't bet on Them.

Frankly, I wouldn't bet on Us either. In eight years, American troops have worn out their welcome. Their very presence now incites opposition, but that's another story. It's Them—the Afghans—I want to talk about.

Afghans are Afghans. They have their own history, their own culture, their own habitual ways of thinking and behaving, all complicated by a modern experience of decades of war, displacement, abject poverty, and incessant meddling by foreign governments near and far—of which the United States has been the most powerful and persistent. Afghans do not think or act like Americans. Yet Americans in power refuse to grasp that inconvenient point.

In the heat of this summer, I went out to the training fields near Kabul where Afghan army recruits are put through their paces, and it was quickly evident just what's getting lost in translation. Our trainers, soldiers from the Illinois National Guard, were masterful. Professional and highly skilled, they were dedicated to carrying out their mission—and doing the job well. They were also big, strong, camouflaged, combat-booted, supersized American men, their bodies swollen by flak jackets and lashed with knives, handguns, and god only knows what else. Any American could be proud of their commitment to tough duty.

The Afghans were puny by comparison: hundreds of little Davids to the overstuffed American Goliaths training them. Keep in mind that Afghan recruits come from a world of desperate poverty. They are almost uniformly malnourished and underweight. Many are no bigger than I am (5'4" and thin)—and some probably not much stronger. Like me, many sag under the weight of a standard-issue flak jacket.

Their American trainers spoke of "upper-body strength deficiency" and prescribed push-ups, because their trainees buckle under the backpacks filled with fifty pounds of equipment and ammo they are expected to carry. All this material must seem absurd to men whose fathers and brothers, wearing only the old cotton shirts and baggy pants of everyday life and carrying battered Russian Kalashnikov rifles, defeated the Red Army two decades ago. American trainers marvel that, freed from heavy equipment and uniforms, Afghan soldiers can run through the mountains all day—as the Taliban guerrillas in fact do with great effect—but the US military is determined to train them for another style of war.

Still, the new recruits turn out for training in the blistering heat of this stony desert landscape, wearing, beneath their heavy uniforms, the smart red, green, and black warm-up outfits intended to encourage them to engage in off-duty exercise. American trainers recognize that recruits regularly wear *all* their gear at once, for fear somebody will steal anything left behind in the barracks, but they take this overdressing as a sign of how much Afghans love the military. My own reading, based on my observations of Afghan life during the years I've spent in that country, is this: it's a sign of how little they trust one another, or the Americans who gave them the snazzy suits. I think it also indicates the obvious: that these impoverished men in a country without work have joined the Afghan National Army for what they can get out of it (and keep or sell)—and that doesn't include democracy or glory.

In the current policy debate about the Afghan War in Washington, Senate Armed Services Committee Chairman Carl Levin wants the Afghans to defend their country. Senator John McCain, the top Republican on the committee, agrees, but says they need even more help from even more Americans. The common ground—the sacred territory President Obama gropes for—is that, whatever else happens, the US must speed up the training of the "Afghan security forces."

American military planners and policymakers proceed as if, with sufficient training, Afghans can be transformed into scale-model, wind-up
American Marines. That is not going to happen. Not now. Not ever. No
matter how many of our leaders concur that it *must* happen—and ever
faster.

"BASIC WARRIOR TRAINING"

So who are these security forces? They include the Afghan National Army
(ANA) and the Afghan National Police (ANP). International forces and
private contractors have been training Afghan recruits for both of them
since 2001. In fact, the determination of Western military planners to
create a national army and police force has been so great that some seem to
have suppressed for years the reports of Canadian soldiers who witnessed
members of the Afghan security forces engaging in a fairly common
pastime, sodomizing young boys.

Current training and mentoring is provided by the US, Great Britain,
France, Canada, Romania, Poland, Mongolia, New Zealand, and Australia,
as well as by the private for-profit contractors MPRI, KBR (formerly a division of Halliburton), Pulau, Paravant, and RONCO.

Almost eight years and counting since the "mentoring" process began,
officers at the Kabul Military Training Center report that the army now
numbers between 88,000 and 92,000 soldiers, depending on who you talk
to; and the basic training course financed and led by Americans, called
"Basic Warrior Training," is turning out 28,800 new soldiers every year,
according to a Kabul Military Training Center "fact sheet." The current
projected "end strength" for the ANA, to be reached in December 2011,
is 134,000 men; but Afghan officers told me they're planning for a force of
200,000, while the Western press often cites 240,000 as the final figure.

The number 400,000 is often mentioned as the supposed end-strength
quota for the combined security forces—an army of 240,000 soldiers and
a police force with 160,000 men. Yet Afghan National Police officials also
speak of a far more inflated figure, 250,000, and they claim that 149,000 men
have already been trained. Police training has always proven problematic,
however, in part because, from the start, the European allies fundamentally disagreed with the Bush administration about what the role of the
Afghan police should be. Germany initiated the training of what it saw

as an unarmed force that would direct traffic, deter crime, and keep civic order for the benefit of the civilian population. The US took over in 2003, handed the task off to a private for-profit military contractor, DynCorp, and proceeded to produce a heavily armed, undisciplined, and thoroughly venal paramilitary force despised by Kabulis and feared by Afghan civilians in the countryside.

Contradicting that widespread public view, an Afghan commanding officer of the ANP assured me that today the police are trained as police, not as a paramilitary auxiliary of the ANA. "But policing is different in Afghanistan," he said, because the police operate in active war zones.

Washington sends mixed messages on this subject. It farms out responsibility for the ANP to a private contractor that hires as mentors retired American law enforcement officers—a Kentucky state trooper, a Texas county lawman, a North Carolina cop, and so on. Yet Washington policymakers continue to couple the police with the army as "the Afghan security forces"—the most basic police rank is "soldier"—in a merger that must influence what DynCorp puts in its training syllabus. At the Afghan National Police training camp outside Kabul, I watched a squad of trainees learn (reluctantly) how to respond to a full-scale ambush. Though they were armed only with red rubber Kalashnikovs, the exercise looked to me much like the military maneuvers I'd witnessed at the army training camp.

Like army training, police training, too, was accelerated months ago to ensure "security" during the run-up to the presidential election. With that goal in mind, DynCorp mentors shrunk the basic police training course from eight weeks to three, after which the police were dispatched to villages all across the country, including areas controlled by the Taliban. After the election, the surviving short-course police "soldiers" were to be brought back to Kabul for the rest of the basic training program. There's no word yet on how many returned.

You have to wonder about the wisdom of rushing out this half-baked product. How would you feel if the police in your community were turned loose, heavily armed, after three weeks of training? And how would you feel if you were given a three-week training course with a rubber gun and then dispatched, with a real one, to defend your country?

Training security forces is not cheap. So far, the estimated cost of training and mentoring the police since 2001 is at least $10 billion. Any reliable figure on the cost of training and mentoring the Afghan army since 2001 is as invisible as the army itself. But the US currently spends some $4 billion a month on military operations in Afghanistan.

THE INVISIBLE MEN

What is there to show for all this remarkably expensive training? Although in Washington they may talk about the 90,000 soldiers in the Afghan National Army, no one has reported actually seeing such an army anywhere in Afghanistan. When 4,000 US Marines were sent into Helmand Province in July to take on the Taliban in what is considered one of its strongholds, accompanying them were only about 600 Afghan security forces, some of whom were police. Why, you might ask, didn't the ANA, 90,000 strong after eight years of training and mentoring, handle Helmand on its own? No explanation has been offered. American and NATO officers often complain that Afghan army units are simply not ready to "operate independently," but no one ever speaks to the simple question: where are they?

My educated guess is that such an army simply does not exist. It may well be true that Afghan men have gone through some version of "Basic Warrior Training" 90,000 times or more. When I was teaching in Afghanistan from 2002 to 2006, I knew men who repeatedly went through ANA training to get the promised Kalashnikov and the pay. Then they went home for a while and often returned some weeks later to enlist again under a different name.

In a country where 40 percent of men are unemployed, joining the ANA for ten weeks is the best game in town. It relieves the poverty of many families every time the man of the family goes back to basic training, but it's a needlessly complicated way to unintentionally deliver such minimal humanitarian aid. Some of these circulating soldiers are aging former mujahideen—the Islamist fundamentalists the US once paid to fight the Soviets—and many are undoubtedly Taliban.

American trainers have taken careful note of the fact that, when ANA soldiers were given leave after basic training to return home with their pay, they generally didn't come back. To foil paycheck scams and decrease soaring rates of desertion, they recently devised a money-transfer system that allows the soldiers to send pay home without ever leaving their base. That sounds like a good idea, but like many expensive American solutions to

Afghan problems, it misses the point. It's not just the money the soldier wants to transfer home, it's himself as well.

Earlier this year, the US training program became slightly more compelling with the introduction of a US-made weapon, the M-16 rifle, which was phased in over four months as a replacement for the venerable Kalashnikov. Even US trainers admit that, in Afghanistan, the Kalashnikov is actually the superior weapon. Light and accurate, it requires no cleaning even in the dust of the high desert, and every man and boy already knows it well. The strange and sensitive M-16, on the other hand, may be more accurate at slightly greater distances, but only if a soldier can keep it clean, while managing to adjust and readjust its notoriously sensitive sights. The struggling soldiers of the ANA may not ace that test, but now that the US military has generously passed on its old M-16s to Afghans, it can buy new ones at taxpayer expense, a prospect certain to gladden the heart of any arms manufacturer. (Incidentally, thanks must go to the Illinois National Guard for risking their lives to make possible such handsome corporate profits.)

As for the police, US-funded training offers a similar revolving door. In Afghanistan, however, it is far more dangerous to be a policeman than a soldier. While soldiers on patrol can slip away, policemen stuck at their posts are killed almost every day. Assigned in small numbers to staff small-town police stations or highway checkpoints, they are sitting ducks for Taliban fighters. As representatives of the now thoroughly discredited government of President Hamid Karzai, the hapless police make handy symbolic targets. British commanders in Helmand Province estimated that 60 percent of Afghan police are on drugs—and little wonder.

In the Pashtun provinces of southern Afghanistan, where the Taliban is strong, recruiting men for the Afghan National Police is a "problem," as an ANP commander told me. Consequently, non-Pashtun police trainees of Hazara, Tajik, Uzbek, or other ethnic backgrounds are dispatched to maintain order in Pashtun territory. They might as well paint targets on their foreheads. The police who accompanied the US Marines into Helmand Province reportedly refused to leave their heavily armed mentors to take up suicidal posts in provincial villages. Some police and army soldiers, when asked by reporters, claimed to be "visiting" Helmand Province only for a "vacation."

TRAINING DAY

In many districts, the police recently supplemented their low pay and demonstrated allegiance to local warlords by stuffing ballot boxes for President Karzai in the presidential election. Consider that but one more indication—like the defection of those great Islamist fundamentalist mujahideen allies the US sponsored in the anti-Soviet jihad of the 1980s, who are now fighting with the Taliban—that no amount of American training, mentoring, or cash will determine who or what Afghans will fight for, if indeed they fight at all.

Afghans are world-famous fighters, in part because they have a knack for gravitating to the winning side, and they're ready to change sides with alacrity until they get it right. Recognizing that Afghans back a winner, US military strategists are now banking on a counterinsurgency strategy that seeks to "clear, hold, and build"—that is, to stick around long enough to win the Afghans over. But it's way too late for that to work. These days, US troops sticking around look ever more like a foreign occupying army and, to the Taliban, like targets.

Recently Karen DeYoung noted in the *Washington Post* that the Taliban now regularly use very sophisticated military techniques—"as if the insurgents had attended something akin to the US Army's Ranger school, which teaches soldiers how to fight in small groups in austere environments." Of course, some of them have attended training sessions which teach them to fight in "austere environments," probably time and time again. If you were a Talib, wouldn't you scout the training being offered to Afghans on the other side? And wouldn't you do it more than once if you could get well paid every time?

Such training is bound to come in handy—as it may have for the Talib policeman who, just last week, bumped off eight other comrades at his police post in Kunduz Province in northern Afghanistan and turned it over to the Taliban. On the other hand, such training can be deadly to American trainers. Take the case of the American trainer who was shot and wounded that same week by one of his trainees. Reportedly, a dispute arose because the trainer was drinking water "in front of locals," while the trainees were fasting for the Muslim holy month of Ramadan.

There is, by the way, plenty of evidence that Taliban fighters get along just fine, fighting fiercely and well without the training lavished on the

ANA and the ANP. Why is it that Afghan Taliban fighters seem so bold and effective, while the Afghan National Police are so dismally corrupt and the Afghan National Army a washout?

When I visited bases and training grounds in July 2009, I heard some American trainers describe their Afghan trainees in the same racist terms once applied to African slaves in the US: lazy, irresponsible, stupid, childish, and so on. That's how Afghan resistance, avoidance, and sabotage look to American eyes. The Taliban fight for something they believe—that their country should be freed from foreign occupation. "Our" Afghans try to get by.

Yet one amazing thing happens to ANA trainees who stick it out for the whole ten weeks of basic training. Their slight bodies begin to fill out a little. They gain more energy and better spirits—all because for the first time in their lives they have enough nutritious food to eat.

Better nutrition notwithstanding—Senator Levin, Senator McCain—"our" Afghans are never going to fight for an American cause, with or without American troops, the way we imagine they should. They're never going to fight with the energy of the Taliban for a national government that we installed against Afghan wishes, then more recently set up to steal another election, and now seem about to ratify in office, despite incontrovertible evidence of flagrant fraud. Why should they? Even if the US could win their minds, their hearts are not in it.

One small warning: don't use the insecurity of the Afghan security forces as an argument for sending yet more American troops to Afghanistan. Aggressive Americans (now numbering 68,000) are likely to be even less successful than reluctant Afghan forces. Afghans want peace, but the *kharaji* (foreign) troops (100,000, if you include US allies in NATO) bring death and destruction wherever they go. Think instead about what you might have won—and could still win—had you spent all those military billions on food. Or maybe agriculture. Or health care. Or a civilian job corps. Is it too late for that now?

9 PAYING OFF THE WARLORDS: ANATOMY OF A CULTURE OF CORRUPTION

By Pratap Chatterjee

Kabul, Afghanistan—Every morning, dozens of trucks laden with diesel from Turkmenistan lumber out of the northern Afghan border town of Hairaton on a two-day trek across the Hindu Kush down to Afghanistan's capital, Kabul. Among the dozens of businesses dispatching these trucks are two extremely well-connected companies—Ghazanfar and Zahid Walid— that helped to swell the election coffers of President Hamid Karzai as well as the family business of his running mate, the country's new vice president, warlord Mohammed Qasim Fahim.

Some of the trucks are on their way to two power stations in the northern part of the capital: a recently refurbished, if inefficient, plant that has served Kabul for a little more than a quarter of a century, and a brand new facility scheduled for completion next year and built with money from the US Agency for International Development (USAID).

Afghan political analysts observe that Ghazanfar and Zahid Walid are striking examples of the multimillion-dollar business conglomerates, financed by American as well as Afghan tax dollars and connected to powerful political figures, that have, since the fall of the Taliban in 2001, emerged as part of a pervasive culture of corruption here. Nasrullah Stanikzai, a professor of law and political science at Kabul University, says of the companies in the pocket of the vice president: "Everybody knows who is Ghazanfar. Everybody knows who is Zahid Walid. The [government elite] directly or indirectly have companies, licenses, and sign contracts. But corruption is not confined just to the Afghans. The international community bears a share of this blame."

Indeed, the tale of the "reconstruction" of Kabul's electricity supply is a classic story of how foreign aid has often served to line the pockets of both international contractors from the donor countries and the local political elite. Unfortunately, these aid-financed projects also generally fail—as the Kabul diesel plants appear destined to—because of a lack of planning and the hard cash to keep them operating.

RISE OF A POWER BROKER

Abdul Hasin and his brother, the vice president, offer a perfect exemplar of the new business elite. The two men are half-brothers, born to the two wives of a well-respected religious cleric from the village of Marz in the Panjshir valley north of Kabul.

In the early 1980s, Fahim, the older brother, joined the mujahideen forces of Ahmed Shah Massoud in the struggle against the Soviet occupation of Afghanistan. In 1992, three years after the Soviet army withdrew in defeat, Fahim was appointed head of intelligence in Afghanistan by the new president Burhanuddin Rabbani in the midst of a fierce and destructive civil war among the victors. When the Taliban took control of the country a few years later, Fahim became the intelligence chief for the Northern Alliance, also led by Massoud, which controlled less than a third of the country. On September 9, 2001, two days before the World Trade Center was attacked, Massoud was assassinated by al Qaeda operatives and Fahim took control of the Northern Alliance, which the US would soon finance and support in its "invasion" of Afghanistan.

A number of popular accounts of that invasion, such as Bob Woodward's book *Bush at War*, suggest that the Central Intelligence Agency directly gave Northern Alliance warlords like Fahim millions of dollars in cold, hard cash to help fight the Taliban in the run-up to the US invasion. "I can take Kabul, I can take Kunduz if you break the [Taliban front] line for me. My guys are ready," Woodward quotes Fahim telling a CIA agent named Gary, after pocketing a million dollars in $100 bills.

Once the Taliban was defeated, Fahim was invited to become vice president in the transitional government led by Hamid Karzai, a position he held for two years. It was at this juncture that Fahim's brothers, notably Abdul Hasin, started to build a business empire—and not long after, good fortune began to rain down on the family in the form of lucrative "reconstruction" contracts.

In January 2002, while Fahim took whirlwind tours of Washington and London, meeting General Tommy Franks, who had commanded US forces during the invasion, and taking the salute from the Coldstream Guards, his younger brother was putting together a business plan. Soon thereafter, Zahid Walid, a company named after Abdul Hasin's older sons, not so surprisingly won a series of lucrative contracts to pour concrete for a NATO base as well as portions of the US embassy being rebuilt in Kabul and that city's airport, which was in a state of disrepair.

On a plot of land in downtown Kabul reportedly "seized" for a song by Fahim, Abdul Hasin also financed the construction of a high-rise building dubbed "Goldpoint," which now houses dozens of jewelry shops. Soon, the company was importing Russian gas, and not long after that, Abdul Hasin set up the Gas Group, a company which ran a plant in the industrial suburb of Tarakhil that marketed bottled gas to households and small businesses.

In the winter of 2006, Zahid Walid won a $12 million contract from the Afghan ministry of energy and water to supply fuel to the old diesel plant in northwest Kabul, according to data published on the website of the government's central procurement agency, Afghanistan Reconstruction and Development Services. In the summer of 2007, the company won another $40 million diesel-supply contract, and last winter it took on a third contract worth $22 million.

On October 19, 2009, I visited Zahid Walid's heavily guarded headquarters in the wealthy Kabul neighborhood of Wazir Akbar Khan, not far from the even more heavily fortified US embassy. There, Ramin Seddiqui, the managing director of the company's diesel-import business, filled me in on another exclusive contract the company had secured from the Afghan government only days before, worth an additional $17 million. Zahid Walid is now to supply diesel fuel to the new 100-megawatt diesel power plant being built by Black & Veatch, a Kansas construction company, with money from USAID.

Most senior Afghan government officials and political figures are loath to discuss how Zahid Walid has won all these contracts—at least publicly. On a recent visit to the Ministry of Commerce, I asked Noor Mohammed Wafa, the general director of oil products and liquid gas, about them. He promptly claimed that he had never even heard of the company. He then shot a glance at my Afghan assistant and said in Dari: "That's Marshal Fahim's company, isn't it?" When I asked whether the rules were different for powerful political figures—as everyone in Kabul knows is the case—Wafa politely denied any suggestion of favoritism in the awarding of import licenses.

In fact, dozens of people assured me in private on my most recent visit to Kabul that favoritism and corruption are the essence of the Karzai government the US has helped "reconstruct" over the last eight years.

A WHITE-ELEPHANT POWER PLANT IN KABUL

While Zahid Walid has won close to $100 million in diesel contracts from the Afghan government in these years, there is hard evidence that the money for this once-needed fuel is now essentially being squandered. Earlier this year, KEC, an Indian company, completed the first of two high voltage power lines from neighboring Central Asian countries that will bring cheap and reliable electricity into the capital.

The initial 220-kilovolt power line from Uzbekistan—a $35 million project—follows the same path as Zahid Walid's diesel trucks over the Hindu Kush. The comparison, however, ends there. True, the Indian engineers who constructed it had to survive the brutal snows in the Salang pass, but they are now done. On the other hand, the truckers continue to take the treacherous daily drive through the tunnel that connects northern Afghanistan to the south, bringing Turkmen diesel to Kabul at twenty-two cents a kilowatt hour. Meanwhile, the Uzbek electricity, traveling effortlessly through KEC's transmission lines, costs the Afghan taxpayer a mere six cents a kilowatt hour.

To add insult to injury, much of the diesel is meant for the USAID power plant at Tarakhil that has become a symbol of the sort of massive and widespread reconstruction waste and abuse that has gone on in this country for years. The plant, built by Black & Veatch, is now projected to cost $300 million, three times the price of similar plants in neighboring Pakistan. In addition, it will only be capable of supplying one-third of the power the Uzbek power line can deliver far less expensively. Nor will the Uzbek line be the only source of cheap electricity. KEC's engineers have broken ground on a second power line—this one from Tajikistan—that will supply 300 megawatts of electricity to Kabul, three times what the Tarakhil plant will produce at a bargain-basement construction cost of $28 million.

"At full capacity, we burn 600,000 liters a day," Jack Currie, the Scottish manager of the Tarakhil plant told me as I toured it in late October 2009. "And just how much will that cost the Afghan taxpayer?" I asked. "Well," replied Currie, "you can assume a dollar a liter of diesel." I quickly calculated and arrived at an annual total of $219 million per year, not including the plant's maintenance costs (estimated at another $60 million a year). Currie looked astonished when I mentioned the figure.

I took these numbers to Mohammed Khan, a member of the Afghan parliament and chair of its energy committee. "Will you approve the funds for this diesel power plant?" I asked. The soft-spoken Khan, a trained electrical engineer who worked for many years in the Kabul Electricity Department, answered simply: "No. Not unless we have an emergency."

So why build a power plant that, in terms of kilowatt hours made available, costs twenty-six times as much as the Indian-built power line? Anwar-ul-Haq Ahadi, Afghan's former finance minister, recalls the process. The idea, he says, originally came from then-US Ambassador to Afghanistan Ronald Neumann, who dreamed it up in April 2007 shortly before he left the country. He apparently envisioned it as a strategic alternative to the Uzbek power line. After all, at that time the repressive Uzbek regime had denied Washington the use of what was seen as a key military base in Central Asia, Karshi-Khanabad, and so functionally kicked US troops out of the country. Naturally, then, it was also seen as an unreliable political partner for the US-backed regime of Hamid Karzai.

Following up, USAID officials told the Karzai government that they could build a diesel plant in Kabul in just over two years for $120 million. It would, the ambassador indicated, be functional just in time for the 2009 elections, allowing Karzai to claim that he had provided power to the electricity-starved capital. The Afghan president readily agreed to the plan, instructing anxious officials at the ministry of finance to approve the scheme in early 2007. He even agreed to put $20 million of Afghan funds into the project—after being assured that the US would pay for the rest.

Over the next two years, while Indian engineers raced the Americans to provide power to Kabul (ultimately winning handily), the ministry of energy and water was having a hard time keeping the lights on during Kabul's harsh winters. And while the city waited for these promised sources of power to come on line, the new political-business elite, with its specially set up companies like Zahid Walid, was winning government-issued contracts to supply diesel to the old Kabul power plant—and making money hand over fist.

Zahid Walid was hardly the only politically well-connected business to clean up: Ghazanfar, a company from Mazar-i-Sharif, also won $17 million in diesel-supply contracts in the winter of 2006–2007, and then an astonishing $78 million in new contracts for 2008–early 2009. Not surprisingly, Ghazanfar turns out to be run by a family that is very close to President Karzai. (One sister, Hosn Banu Ghazanfar, is the women's minister and a brother is a member of parliament.)

In March 2009, the Ghazanfars opened a new bank in the capital, plastering the city with giant billboard advertisements featuring a cascade of gold coins. Less than six months later, the bank wrote out a $2 million interest-free loan to Karzai for his election campaign, paying back the favors his government had done for them over the previous three years.

AFGHANISTAN AS A PATRONAGE MACHINE

In the time of writing, in November 2009, Mohammed Qasim Fahim is shortly to be sworn in as the next vice-president of the new government of Afghanistan. Under an agreement with USAID, this new government is required to spend Afghan money to buy yet more diesel for the Tarakhil power plant, which in turn will put money exclusively and directly into the vice president's brother's pocket.

Hamid Jalil, the aid coordinator for the Ministry of Finance, points out that wasting money on unnecessary projects like Tarakhil has helped to hobble Afghanistan's progress in the last eight years. "The donor projects undermine the legitimacy of the government and do not allow us to build capacity," he says, adding in the weary tone you often hear in Kabul today, "corruption is everywhere in post-conflict countries like ours."

Former Afghan finance minister Ashraf Ghani summed up the whole profitably corrupt system that has run Afghanistan into a cul-de-sac this way. "It's not crazy, it's absurd," he says. "Crazy is when you don't know what you're doing. Absurd is when you don't provide a sense of ownership and a sense of sustainability."

10 HOW THE US FUNDS THE TALIBAN

By Aram Roston

On October 29, 2001, while the Taliban's rule over Afghanistan was under assault, the regime's ambassador in Islamabad gave a chaotic press conference in front of several dozen reporters sitting on the grass. On the Taliban diplomat's right sat his interpreter, Ahmad Rateb Popal, a man with an imposing presence. Like the ambassador, Popal wore a black turban, and he had a huge bushy beard. He had a black patch over his right eye socket, a prosthetic left arm and a deformed right hand, the result of injuries from an explosives mishap during an old operation against the Soviets in Kabul.

But Popal was more than just a former mujahideen. In 1988, a year before the Soviets fled Afghanistan, Popal had been charged in the United States with conspiring to import more than a kilo of heroin. Court records show he was released from prison in 1997.

Flash forward to 2009, and Afghanistan is ruled by Popal's cousin President Hamid Karzai. Popal has cut his huge beard down to a neatly trimmed one and has become an immensely wealthy businessman, along with his brother Rashid Popal, who in a separate case pleaded guilty to a heroin charge in 1996 in Brooklyn. The Popal brothers control the huge Watan Group in Afghanistan, a consortium engaged in telecommunications, logistics, and, most important, security. Watan Risk Management, the Popals' private military arm, is one of the few dozen private security companies in Afghanistan. One of Watan's enterprises, key to the war effort, is protecting convoys of Afghan trucks heading from Kabul to Kandahar, carrying American supplies.

Welcome to the wartime contracting bazaar in Afghanistan. It is a virtual carnival of improbable characters and shady connections, with former CIA officials and ex-military officers joining hands with former Taliban and mujahideen to collect US government funds in the name of the war effort.

In this grotesque carnival, the US military's contractors are forced to pay suspected insurgents to protect American supply routes. It is an accepted fact of the military logistics operation in Afghanistan that the US government funds the very forces American troops are fighting. And it is a deadly irony, because these funds add up to a huge amount of money for the Taliban. "It's a big part of their income," one of the top Afghan government security officials told *The Nation* in an interview. In fact, US military officials in Kabul estimate that a minimum of 10 percent of the Pentagon's logistics contracts—hundreds of millions of dollars—consists of payments to insurgents.

Understanding how this situation came to pass requires untangling two threads. The first is the insider dealing that determines who wins and who loses in Afghan business, and the second is the troubling mechanism by which "private security" ensures that the US supply convoys traveling these ancient trade routes aren't ambushed by insurgents.

A good place to pick up the first thread is with a small firm awarded a US military logistics contract worth hundreds of millions of dollars: NCL Holdings. Like the Popals' Watan Risk, NCL is a licensed security company in Afghanistan.

What NCL Holdings is most notorious for in Kabul contracting circles, though, is the identity of its chief principal, Hamed Wardak. He is the young American son of Afghanistan's current defense minister, General Abdul Rahim Wardak, who was a leader of the mujahideen against the Soviets. Hamed Wardak has plunged into business as well as policy. He was raised and schooled in the United States, graduating as valedictorian from Georgetown University in 1997. He earned a Rhodes scholarship and interned at the neoconservative think tank the American Enterprise Institute. That internship was to play an important role in his life, for it was at AEI that he forged alliances with some of the premier figures in American conservative foreign policy circles, such as the late Ambassador Jeane Kirkpatrick.

Wardak incorporated NCL in the United States early in 2007, although the firm may have operated in Afghanistan before then. It made sense to set up shop in Washington, because of Wardak's connections there. On NCL's advisory board, for example, is Milton Bearden, a well-known former CIA officer. Bearden is an important voice on Afghanistan issues; in October he was a witness before the Senate Foreign Relations Committee, where Senator John Kerry, the chair, introduced him as "a legendary former CIA case officer and a clearheaded thinker and writer." It is not every defense contracting company that has such an influential adviser.

But the biggest deal that NCL got—the contract that brought it into Afghanistan's major leagues—was Host Nation Trucking. In early 2009 the firm, with no apparent trucking experience, was named one of the six companies that would handle the bulk of US trucking in Afghanistan, bringing supplies to the web of bases and remote outposts scattered across the country.

At first the contract was large but not gargantuan. And then that suddenly changed, like an immense garden coming into bloom. Over the summer of 2009, citing the coming "surge" and a new doctrine, "Money as a Weapons System," the US military expanded the contract 600 percent for NCL and the five other companies. The contract documentation warns of dire consequences if more is not spent: "service members will not get food, water, equipment, and ammunition they require." Each of the military's six trucking contracts was bumped up to $360 million, or a total of nearly $2.2 billion. Put it in this perspective: this single two-year effort to hire Afghan trucks and truckers was worth 10 percent of the annual Afghan gross domestic product. NCL, the firm run by the defense minister's well-connected son, had struck pure contracting gold.

Host Nation Trucking does indeed keep the US military efforts alive in Afghanistan. "We supply everything the army needs to survive here," one American trucking executive told me. "We bring them their toilet paper, their water, their fuel, their guns, their vehicles." The epicenter is Bagram Air Base, just an hour north of Kabul, from which virtually everything in Afghanistan is trucked to the outer reaches of what the Army calls "the Battlespace"—that is, the entire country. Parked near Entry Control Point 3, the trucks line up, shifting gears and sending up clouds of dust as they prepare for their various missions across the country.

The real secret to trucking in Afghanistan is ensuring security on the perilous roads, controlled by warlords, tribal militias, insurgents, and Taliban commanders. The American executive I talked to was fairly specific about it: "The Army is basically paying the Taliban not to shoot at them. It is Department of Defense money." That is something everyone seems to agree on.

Mike Hanna is the project manager for a trucking company called Afghan American Army Services. The company, which still operates in Afghanistan, had been trucking for the United States for years but lost out in the Host Nation Trucking contract that NCL won. Hanna explained the security realities quite simply: "You are paying the people in the local areas—some are warlords, some are politicians in the police force—to move your trucks through."

Hanna explained that the prices charged are different, depending on the route: "We're basically being extorted. Where you don't pay, you're going to get attacked. We just have our field guys go down there, and they pay off who they need to." Sometimes, he says, the extortion fee is high, and sometimes it is low. "Moving ten trucks, it is probably $800 per truck to move through an area. It's based on the number of trucks and what you're carrying. If you have fuel trucks, they are going to charge you more. If you have dry trucks, they're not going to charge you as much. If you are carrying MRAPs or Humvees, they are going to charge you more."

Hanna says it is just a necessary evil. "If you tell me not to pay these insurgents in this area, the chances of my trucks getting attacked increase exponentially."

Whereas in Iraq the private security industry has been dominated by US and global firms like Blackwater, operating as de facto arms of the US government, in Afghanistan there are lots of local players as well. As a result, the industry in Kabul is far more dog-eat-dog. "Every warlord has his security company," is the way one executive explained it to me.

In theory, private security companies in Kabul are heavily regulated, although the reality is different. Thirty-nine companies had licenses until September, when another dozen were granted licenses. Many licensed companies are politically connected: just as NCL is owned by the son of the defense minister and Watan Risk Management is run by President Karzai's cousins, the Asia Security Group is controlled by Hashmat Karzai, another relative of the president. The company has blocked off an entire street in the expensive Sherpur District. Another security firm is controlled by the parliamentary speaker's son, sources say. And so on.

In the same way, the Afghan trucking industry, key to logistics operations, is often tied to important figures and tribal leaders. One major hauler in Afghanistan, Afghan International Trucking (AIT), paid $20,000 a month in kickbacks to a US Army contracting official, according to the official's plea agreement in US court in August. AIT is a very well-connected firm: it is run by the twenty-five-year-old nephew of General Baba Jan, a former Northern Alliance commander and later a Kabul police chief. In an interview, Baba Jan, a cheerful and charismatic leader, insisted he had nothing to do with his nephew's corporate enterprise.

But the heart of the matter is that insurgents are getting paid for safe passage because there are few other ways to bring goods to the combat outposts and forward operating bases where soldiers need them. By definition, many outposts are situated in hostile terrain, in the southern parts of Afghanistan. The security firms don't really protect convoys of American military goods here, because they simply can't; they need the Taliban's cooperation.

One of the big problems for the companies that ship American military supplies across the country is that they are banned from arming themselves with any weapon heavier than a rifle. That makes them ineffective for battling Taliban attacks on a convoy. "They are shooting the drivers from 3,000 feet away with PKMs," a trucking company executive in Kabul told me. "They are using RPGs [rocket-propelled grenades] that will blow up an up-armed vehicle. So the security companies are tied up. Because of the rules, security companies can only carry AK-47s, and that's just a joke. I carry an AK—and that's just to shoot myself if I have to!"

The rules are there for a good reason: to guard against devastating collateral damage by private security forces. Still, as Hanna of Afghan American Army Services points out, "An AK-47 versus a rocket-propelled grenade—you are going to lose!" That said, at least one of the Host Nation Trucking companies has tried to do battle instead of paying off insurgents and warlords. It is a US-owned firm called Four Horsemen International. Instead of providing payments, it has tried to fight off attackers. And it has paid the price in lives, with horrendous casualties. FHI, like many other firms, refused to talk publicly; but I've been told by insiders in the security industry that FHI's convoys are attacked on virtually every mission.

For the most part, the security firms do as they must to survive. A veteran American manager in Afghanistan who has worked there as both a soldier and a private security contractor in the field told me, "What we are doing is paying warlords associated with the Taliban, because none of our security elements is able to deal with the threat." He's an Army veteran with years of Special Forces experience, and he's not happy about what's being done. He says that at a minimum American military forces should try to learn more about who is getting paid off.

"Most escorting is done by the Taliban," an Afghan private security official told me. He's a Pashto and former mujahideen commander who has his finger on the pulse of the military situation and the security industry. And he works with one of the trucking companies carrying US supplies. "Now the government is so weak," he added, "everyone is paying the Taliban."

To Afghan trucking officials, this is barely even something to worry about. One woman I met was an extraordinary entrepreneur who had built up a trucking business in this male-dominated field. She told me the security company she had hired dealt directly with Taliban leaders in the south. Paying the Taliban leaders meant they would send along an escort to ensure that no other insurgents would attack. In fact, she said, they just needed two armed Taliban vehicles. "Two Taliban is enough," she told me. "One in the front and one in the back." She shrugged. "You cannot work otherwise. Otherwise it is not possible."

Which leads us back to the case of Watan Risk, the firm run by Ahmad Rateb Popal and Rashid Popal, the Karzai family relatives and former drug dealers. Watan is known to control one key stretch of road that all the truckers use: the strategic route to Kandahar called Highway 1. Think of it as the road to the war—to the south and to the west. If the Army wants to get supplies down to Helmand, for example, the trucks must make their way through Kandahar.

Watan Risk, according to seven different security and trucking company officials, is the sole provider of security along this route. The reason is simple: Watan is allied with the local warlord who controls the road. Watan's company website is quite impressive, and claims its personnel "are diligently screened to weed out all ex-militia members, supporters of the Taliban, or individuals with loyalty to warlords, drug barons, or any other group opposed to international support of the democratic process." Whatever screening methods it uses, Watan's secret weapon to protect American supplies heading through Kandahar is a man named Commander Ruhullah. Said to be a handsome man in his 40s, Ruhullah has an oddly high-pitched voice. He wears traditional *salwar kameez* and a Rolex watch. He rarely, if ever, associates with Westerners. He commands a large group of irregular fighters with no known government affiliation, and his name, security officials tell me, inspires obedience or fear in villages along the road.

It is a dangerous business, of course: until last spring Ruhullah had competition—a one-legged warlord named Commander Abdul Khaliq. He was killed in an ambush.

So Ruhullah is the surviving road warrior for that stretch of highway. According to witnesses, he works like this: he waits until there are hundreds of trucks ready to convoy south down the highway. Then he gets his men together, setting them up in 4x4s and pickups. Witnesses say he does not limit his arsenal to AK-47s but uses any weapons he can get. His chief weapon is his reputation. And for that, Watan is paid royally, collecting a fee for each truck that passes through his corridor. The American trucking official told me that Ruhullah "charges $1,500 per truck to go to Kandahar. Just 300 kilometers."

It's hard to pinpoint what this is, exactly—security, extortion, or a form of "insurance." Then there is the question, does Ruhullah have ties to the Taliban? That's impossible to know. As an American private security veteran familiar with the route said, "He works both sides . . . whatever is most profitable. He's the main commander. He's got to be involved with the Taliban. How much, no one knows."

Even NCL, the company owned by Hamed Wardak, pays. Two sources with direct knowledge tell me that NCL sends its portion of US logistics goods in Watan's and Ruhullah's convoys. Sources say NCL is billed $500,000 per month for Watan's services. To underline the point: NCL, operating on a $360 million contract from the US military, and owned by the Afghan defense minister's son, is paying millions per year from those funds to a company owned by President Karzai's cousins, for protection.

Hamed Wardak wouldn't return my phone calls. Milton Bearden, the former CIA officer affiliated with the company, wouldn't speak with me either. There's nothing wrong with Bearden engaging in business in Afghanistan, but disclosure of his business interests might have been expected when testifying on US policy in Afghanistan and Pakistan. After all, NCL stands to make or lose hundreds of millions based on the whims of US policymakers.

It is certainly worth asking why NCL, a company with no known trucking experience, and little security experience to speak of, would win a contract worth $360 million. Plenty of Afghan insiders are asking questions. "Why would the US government give him a contract if he is the son of the minister of defense?" That's what Mahmoud Karzai asked me. He is the brother of President Karzai, and he himself has been treated in the press as a poster boy for access to government officials. The *New York Times* even profiled him in a highly critical piece. In his defense, Karzai emphasized that he, at least, has refrained from US government or Afghan government contracting. He pointed out, as others have, that Hamed Wardak had little security or trucking background before his company received security and trucking contracts from the Defense Department. "That's a questionable business practice," he said. "They shouldn't give it to him. How come that's not questioned?"

I did get the opportunity to ask General Wardak, Hamed's father, about it. He is quite dapper, although he is no longer the debonair "Gucci commander" Bearden once described. I asked Wardak about his son and NCL. "I've tried to be straightforward and correct and fight corruption all my life," the defense minister said. "This has been something people have tried to use against me, so it has been painful."

Wardak would speak only briefly about NCL. The issue seems to have produced a rift with his son. "I was against it from the beginning, and that's why we have not talked for a long time. I have never tried to support him or to use my power or influence so that he should benefit."

When I told Wardak that his son's company had a US contract worth as much as $360 million, he did a double take. "This is impossible," he said. "I do not believe this."

I believed the general when he said he really didn't know what his son was up to. But cleaning up what look like insider deals may be easier than the next step: shutting down the money pipeline going from DoD contracts to potential insurgents.

Two years ago, a top Afghan security official told me, Afghanistan's intelligence service, the National Directorate of Security, had alerted the

American military to the problem. The NDS delivered what I'm told are "very detailed" reports to the Americans explaining how the Taliban are profiting from protecting convoys of US supplies.

The Afghan intelligence service even offered a solution: what if the United States were to take the tens of millions paid to security contractors and instead set up a dedicated and professional convoy support unit to guard its logistics lines? The suggestion went nowhere.

The bizarre fact is that the practice of buying the Taliban's protection is not a secret. I asked Colonel David Haight, who commands the Third Brigade of the Tenth Mountain Division, about it. After all, part of Highway 1 runs through his area of operations. What did he think about security companies paying off insurgents? "The American soldier in me is repulsed by it," he said in an interview in his office at FOB Shank in Logar Province. "But I know that it is what it is: essentially paying the enemy, saying, 'Hey, don't hassle me.' I don't like it, but it is what it is."

As a military official in Kabul explained contracting in Afghanistan overall, "We understand that across the board 10 percent to 20 percent goes to the insurgents. My intel guy would say it is closer to 10 percent. Generally it is happening in logistics."

In a statement to *The Nation* about Host Nation Trucking, Colonel Wayne Shanks, the chief public affairs officer for the international forces in Afghanistan, said that military officials are "aware of allegations that procurement funds may find their way into the hands of insurgent groups, but we do not directly support or condone this activity, if it is occurring." He added that, despite oversight, "the relationships between contractors and their subcontractors, as well as between subcontractors and others in their operational communities, are not entirely transparent."

In any case, the main issue is not that the US military is turning a blind eye to the problem. Many officials acknowledge what is going on while also expressing a deep disquiet about the situation. The trouble is that—as with so much in Afghanistan—the United States doesn't seem to know how to fix it.

11 REMEMBER THE WOMEN?

By Ann Jones

Women are made for homes or graves.
–Afghan saying

General Stanley McChrystal says he needs more American troops to salvage something like winning in Afghanistan and restore the country to "normal life." Influential senators want to increase spending to train more soldiers for the Afghan National Army and Police. American non-profit organization the Feminist Majority Foundation recently backed off a call for more troops, but it continues to warn against US withdrawal as an abandonment of Afghan women and girls. Nearly everyone assumes troops bring greater security; and whether your touchstone is military victory, national interest, or the welfare of women and girls, "security" seems a good thing.

I confess that I agonize over competing proposals now commanding President Obama's attention because I've spent years in Afghanistan working with women, and I'm on their side. When the Feminist Majority Foundation argues that withdrawing American forces from Afghanistan will return the Taliban to power and women to house arrest, I see in my mind's eye the faces of women I know and care about. Yet an unsentimental look at the record reveals that for all the fine talk of women's rights since the US invasion, equal rights for Afghan women have been illusory all along, a polite feel-good fiction that helped to sell the American enterprise at home and cloak in respectability the misbegotten government we installed in Kabul. That it is a fiction is borne out by recent developments in Afghanistan—President Karzai's approving a new family law worthy of the Taliban, and American acquiescence in Karzai's new law and, initially, his theft of the presidential election—and by the systematic intimidation, murder, or exile of one Afghan woman after another who behaves as if her rights were real and worth fighting for.

Last summer in Kabul, where "security" already suffocates anything remotely suggesting normal life, I asked an Afghan colleague at an international NGO if she was ever afraid. I had learned of threatening phone calls and night letters posted on the gates of the compound, targeting Afghan women who work within. Three of our colleagues in another city had been kidnapped by the militia of a warlord, formerly a member of the Karzai government, and at the time, as we learned after their release, were being beaten, tortured, and threatened with death if they continued to work.

"Fear?" my colleague said. "Yes. We live with fear. In our work here with women we are always under threat. Personally, I work every day in fear, hoping to return safely at the end of the day to my home. To my child and my husband."

"And the future?" I said. "What do you worry about?"

"I think about the upcoming election," she said. "I fear that nothing will change. I fear that everything will stay the same."

Then Karzai gazetted the Shiite Personal Status Law, and it was suddenly clear that even as we were hoping for the best, everything had actually grown much worse for women.

Why is this important? At this critical moment, as Obama tries to weigh options against our national security interests, his advisers can't be bothered with—as one US military officer put it to me—"the trivial fate of women." As for some hypothetical moral duty to protect the women of Afghanistan—that's off the table. Yet it is precisely that dismissive attitude, shared by Afghan and many American men alike, that may have put America's whole Afghan enterprise wrong in the first place. Early on, Kofi Annan, then United Nations secretary general, noted that the condition of Afghan women was "an affront to all standards of dignity, equality and humanity."

Annan took the position, set forth in 2000 in the landmark UN Security Council Resolution 1325, that real conflict resolution, reconstruction, and lasting peace cannot be achieved without the full participation of women every step of the way. Karzai gave lip service to the idea, saying in 2002,

"We are determined to work to improve the lot of women after all their suffering under the narrow-minded and oppressive rule of the Taliban." But he has done no such thing. And the die had already been cast: of the 23 Afghan notables invited to take part in the Bonn Conference in December 2001, only two were women. Among ministers appointed to the new Karzai government, there were only two; one, the minister for women's affairs, was warned not to do "too much."

The Bonn agreement expressed "appreciation to the Afghan mujahidin who . . . have defended the independence, territorial integrity and national unity of the country and have played a major role in the struggle against terrorism and oppression, and whose sacrifice has now made them both heroes of jihad and champions of peace, stability and reconstruction of their beloved homeland, Afghanistan." On the other hand, their American- and Saudi-sponsored "sacrifice" had also made many of them war criminals in the eyes of their countrymen. Most Afghans surveyed between 2002 and 2004 by the Afghan Independent Human Rights Commission thought the leaders of the mujahideen were war criminals who should be brought to justice (75 percent) and removed from public office (90 percent). The muja- hideen, after all, were Islamist extremists just like the Taliban, though less disciplined than the Taliban, who had risen up to curb the violent excesses of the mujahideen and then imposed excesses of their own. That's the part American officials seem unwilling to admit: that the mujahideen warlords of the Karzai government and the oppressive Taliban are brothers under the skin. From the point of view of women today, America's friends and America's enemies in Afghanistan are the same kind of guys.

Though women were excluded from the Bonn process, they did seem to make strides in the first years after the fall of the Taliban. In 2004 a new constitution declared, "The citizens of Afghanistan—whether man or woman—have equal rights and duties before the law." Westerners greeted that language as a confirmation of gender equality, and to this day women's "equal rights" are routinely cited in Western media as evidence of great progress. Yet not surprisingly, Afghan officials often interpret the article differently. To them, having "equal rights and duties" is noth- ing like being equal. The first chief justice of the Afghan Supreme Court, formerly a mullah in a Pakistani madrassa, once explained to me that men have a right to work while women have a right to obey their husbands.

The judiciary—an ultraconservative, inadequate, incompetent, and notoriously corrupt branch of government—interprets the constitution by its own lights. And the great majority of women across the country, knowing little or nothing of rights, live now much as they did under the Taliban—except back then there were no bombs.

In any case, the constitution provides that no law may contravene the principles of Sharia law. In effect, mullahs and judges have always retained the power to decide at any moment what "rights" women may enjoy, or not; and being poorly educated, they're likely to factor into the judgment their own idiosyncratic notions of Sharia, plus tribal customary laws and the size of proffered bribes. Thus, although some women still bravely exercise liberty and work with some success to improve women's condition, it should have been clear from the get-go that Afghan women possess no inalienable rights at all. Western legal experts who train Afghan judges and lawyers in "the law" as we conceive it often express frustration that Afghans just don't get it; Afghan judges think the same of them.

The paper foundations of Afghan women's rights go beyond national law to include the Universal Declaration of Human Rights, the International Treaty of Civil and Political Rights, and the Convention on the Elimination of All Forms of Discrimination Against Women (CEDAW). All these international agreements that delineate and establish human rights around the world were quickly ratified by the Karzai government. CEDAW, however, requires ratifying governments to submit periodic reports on their progress in eliminating discrimination; Afghanistan's first report, due in 2004, hasn't appeared yet. That's one more clue to the Karzai government's real attitude toward women—like Karzai's sequestration of his own wife, a doctor with much-needed skills who is kept locked up at home.

Given this background, there should have been no surprise when President Karzai first signed off in March 2009 on the Shiite Personal Status Law or, as it became known in the Western press, the Marital Rape Law. The bill had been percolating in the ultraconservative Ministry of Justice ever since the Iranian-backed Ayatollah Asif Mohseni submitted it in 2007. Then in February 2008 Karzai apparently saw the chance to swap passage of the SPSL for the votes of the Shiites—that is, the Hazara minority, 15–20 percent of the population. It was just one of many deals Karzai consolidated as he kept to the palace while rival presidential candidates stomped the countryside. The SPSL passed without alteration through the Parliamentary Judicial Committee, another little bunch of ultraconservative men. When it reached the floor of Parliament, it was too late to object. Some women members succeeded in getting the marriageable age for girls—age nine— revised to sixteen. Calling it victory, they settled for that. The Supreme Court reviewed the bill and pronounced it constitutionally correct on grounds the justices did not disclose.

The rights Afghan women stood to lose on paper and in real life were set forth in the SPSL. Parliamentarian Shinkai Karokhail alerted a reporter at the *Guardian*, and the law was denounced around the world for legalizing marital rape by authorizing a husband to withhold food from a wife who fails to provide sexual service at least once every four days. (The interval assumes the husband has four wives, a practice permitted by Islam and legalized by this legislation.) But that's not all the law does. It also denies or severely limits women's rights to inherit, divorce, or have guardian- ship of their own children. It forbids women to marry without permission and legalizes forced marriage. It legalizes marriage to and rape of minors. It gives men control of all their female relatives. It denies women the right to leave home except for "legitimate purposes"—in effect giving men the power to deny women access to work, education, healthcare, voting, and whatever they please. It generally treats women as property, and it considers rape of women or minors outside marriage as a property crime, requiring restitution to be made to the owner, usually the father or husband, rather than a crime against the victim. All these provisions are contained in twenty-six articles of the original bill that have been rendered into English and analyzed by Western legal experts. No doubt other regressive rules will be discovered if the 223 additional articles of the law ever appear in English.

In April 2009 a few women parliamentarians spoke out against the law. A group of women, estimated to number about 300, staged a peaceful protest in the street, protected by Kabul's police officers from an angry mob of hundreds of men who pelted them with obscenities and stones, shouting, "Death to the enemies of Islam!" Under pressure from international diplo- mats—President Obama called the law "abhorrent"—Karzai withdrew it for review. The international press reported the women's victory. In June, when a large group of women MPs and activists met with Karzai, he assured them the bill had been amended and would be submitted to Parliament again after the elections.

Instead, on July 27, 2009, without public announcement, Karzai entered the SPSL, slightly revised but with principal provisions intact, into the official gazette, thereby making it law. Apparently he was betting that with the presidential election only three weeks away, the United States and its allies would not complain again. After all, they had about $500 million (at least half of that American money) riding on a "credible" outcome; and they couldn't afford the cost of a run-off or the political limbo of an interregnum. In August, Brad Adams, Asia director of Human Rights Watch, observed that such "barbaric laws were supposed to have been relegated to the past with the overthrow of the Taliban in 2001, yet Karzai has revived them and given them his official stamp of approval." No American official said a word.

But what about all the women parliamentarians so often cited as evidence of the progress of Afghan women? With 17 percent of the upper house and 27 percent of the lower—85 women in all—you'd think they could have blocked the SPSL. But that didn't happen, for many reasons. Many women parliamentarians are mere extensions of the warlords who financed their campaigns and tell them how to vote: always in opposition to women's rights. Most non-Shiite women took little interest in the bill, believing that it applied only to the Shiite minority. Although Hazara women have long been the freest in the country and the most active in public life, some of them argued that it is better to have a bad law than none at all because, as one Hazara MP told me, "without a written law, men can do whatever they want."

The human rights division of the UN's Assistance Mission in Afghanistan (UNAMA) published a report in early July 2009, before the SPSL became law, documenting the worsening position of Afghan women, the rising violence against them, and the silence of international and Afghan officials who could defend them. The researchers' most surprising finding is this: considering the risks of life outside the home and the support women receive within it, "there is no clear distinction between rural and urban women." Commentators on Afghanistan, myself included, have assumed—somewhat snobbishly, it now appears—that while illiterate women in the countryside might be treated no better than animals, educated urban Afghan women blaze a higher trail. The debacle of the Shiite Personal Status Law explodes that myth.

The UNAMA report attributes women's worsening position in Afghan society to the violence the war engenders on two domestic fronts: the public stage and the home. The report is dedicated to the memory of Sitara Achakzai, a member of the Kandahar Provincial Council and outspoken advocate of women's rights, who was shot to death on April 12, 2009, soon after being interviewed by the UNAMA researchers. She "knew her life was in danger," they report. "But like many other Afghan women such as Malalai Kakar, the highest-ranking female police officer in Kandahar killed in September 2008, Sitara Achakzai had consciously decided to keep fighting to end the abuse of Afghan women." Malalai Kakar, 40, mother of six, had headed a team of ten policewomen handling cases of domestic violence.

In 2005 Kim Sengupta, a reporter with the London *Independent*, interviewed five Afghan women activists; by October 2008 three of them had been murdered. A fourth, Zarghuna Kakar (no relation to Malalai), a member of the Kandahar Provincial Council, had left the country after she and her family were attacked and her husband was killed. She said she had pleaded with Ahmed Wali Karzai, head of the Kandahar Provincial Council, for protection; but he told her she "should have thought about what may happen" before she stood for election. Kakar told the reporter, "It was his brother [President Karzai], the Americans, and the British who told us that we women should get involved in political life. Of course, now I wish I hadn't."

Women learn to pull their punches. MPs in Kabul confessed that they are afraid of the fundamentalist warlords who control the Parliament, so they censor themselves and keep silent. One said, "Most of the time women don't dare even say a word about sensitive Islamic issues, because they are afraid of being labeled as blasphemous." Many women MPs have publicly declared their intention to quit at the end of the term. Women journalists also told UNAMA that they "refrain from criticizing warlords and other power brokers, or covering topics that are deemed contentious such as women's rights."

Other women targeted for attack are civil servants, employees of international and national organizations, including the UN, healthcare workers, and women in "immoral" professions—which include acting, singing, appearing on television, and journalism. When popular Tolo TV presenter Shaima Rezayee, twenty-four, was forced out of her job in 2005, she said "things are not getting better . . . We have made some gains, but there are a lot of people who want to take it all back. They are not even Taliban, they are here in Kabul." Soon after, she was shot and killed. Zakia Zaki, thirty-five, a teacher and radio journalist who produced programs on women's rights, was shot to death in her home in Parwan Province on June 6, 2007. Actress Parwin Mushtakhel fled the country last spring after her husband was gunned down outside their house, punished for his failure to keep her confined. When the Taliban fell, she thought things were getting better, but "the atmosphere has changed; day by day women can work less and less." Setara Hussainzada, the singer from Herat who appeared on the Afghan version of *American Idol* (and in the documentary *Afghan Star*) also fled for her life.

Threats against women in public life are intended to make them go home—to "unliberate" themselves through voluntary house arrest. But if public life is dangerous, so is life at home. Most Afghan women—87 percent, according to Unifem—are beaten on a regular basis. The UNAMA researchers looked into the unmentionable subject of rape and found it to be "an everyday occurrence in all parts of the country" and "a human rights problem of profound proportions." Outside marriage, the rapists are often members or friends of the family. Young girls forced to marry old men are raped by the old man's brothers and sons. Women and children—young boys are also targets—are raped by people who have charge of them: police, prison guards, soldiers, orphanage or hospital staff members. The female victims of rape are mostly between the ages of seven and thirty; many are between ten and twenty, but some are as young as three; and most women are dead by forty-two.

Women rarely tell anyone, because the blame and shame of rape falls on them. Customary law permits an accused rapist to make restitution to the victim's father, but because the question of consent does not figure in the law of sexual relations, the victim is guilty of *zina*, or adultery, and can be punished accordingly: sent to jail or murdered by family members to preserve family honor. The great majority of women and girls in prison at any time are charged with *zina*; most have been raped and/or have run away from home to escape violence. It's probably safe to say, in the absence of statistics, that police—who, incidentally, are trained by the American for-profit contractor DynCorp—spend more time tracking down runaway women and girls than real criminals. Rapists, on the other hand, as

UNAMA investigators found, are often "directly linked to power brokers who are, effectively, above the law and enjoy immunity from arrest as well as immunity from social condemnation." Last year Karzai pardoned political thugs who had gang-raped a woman before witnesses, using a bayonet, and who had somehow been convicted despite their good connections. UNAMA researchers conclude: "The current reality is that . . . women are denied their most fundamental human rights and risk further violence in the course of seeking justice for crimes perpetrated against them." For women, "human rights are values, standards, and entitlements that exist only in theory and at times, not even on paper."

Caught in the maelstrom of personal, political, and military violence, Afghan women worry less about rights than security. But they complain that the men who plan the country's future define "security" in ways that have nothing to do with them. The conventional wisdom, which I have voiced myself, holds that without security, development cannot take place. Hence, our troops must be fielded in greater numbers, and Afghan troops trained faster, and private for-profit military contractors hired at fabulous expense, all to bring security. But the rule doesn't hold in Afghanistan, precisely because of that equation of "security" with the presence of armed men. Wherever troops advance in Afghanistan, women are caught in the cross-fire, killed, wounded, forced to flee or locked up once again, just as they were in the time of the Taliban. Suggesting an alternative to the "major misery" of warfare, Sweden's former defense minister Thage Peterson calls for Swedish soldiers to leave the "military adventure" in Afghanistan while civilians stay to help rebuild the country. But Sweden's soldiers are few, and its aid organizations among the best in the world. For the United States even to lean toward such a plan would mean reasserting civilian control of the military and restoring the American aid program (USAID), hijacked by private for-profit contractors: two goals worth fighting for.

Today, most American so-called development aid is delivered not by USAID, but by the military itself through a system of Provincial Reconstruction Teams (PRTs), another faulty idea of former defense secretary Donald Rumsfeld. Soldiers, unqualified as aid workers and already busy soldiering, now shmooze with village "elders" (often the wrong ones) and bring "development," usually a costly road convenient to the PRT base, impossible for Afghans to maintain and inaccessible to women locked up at home. Recent research conducted by respected Afghanistan hands found that this aid actually fuels "massive corruption"; it fails to win hearts and minds not because we spend too little but because we spend too much, too fast, without a clue. Meanwhile, the Taliban bring the things Afghans say they need—better security, better governance, and quick, hard-edged justice. US government investigators are looking into allegations that aid funds appropriated for women's projects have been diverted to PRTs for this more important work of winning hearts and minds with tarmac. But the greatest problem with routing aid through the military is this: what passes for development is delivered from men to men, affirming in the strongest possible terms the misogynist conviction that women do not matter. You'll recognize it as the same belief that, in the Obama administration's strategic reappraisal of Afghanistan, pushed women off the table.

So there's no point talking about how women and girls might be affected by the strategic military options remaining on Obama's plate. None of them bode well for women. To send more troops is to send more violence. To withdraw is to invite the Taliban. To stay the same is not possible, now that Karzai has stolen the election in plain sight and made a mockery of American pretensions to an interest in anything but our own skin and our own pocketbook. But while men plan the onslaught of more men, it's worth remembering what "normal life" once looked like in Afghanistan, well before the soldiers came. In the 1960s and 70s, before the Soviet invasion—when half the country's doctors, more than half the civil servants and three-quarters of the teachers were women—a peaceful Afghanistan advanced slowly into the modern world through the efforts of all its people. What changed all that was not only the violence of war but the accession to power of the most backward men in the country: first the Taliban, now the mullahs and mujahideen of the fraudulent, corrupt, Western-designed government that stands in opposition to "normal life" as it is lived in the developed world and was once lived in their own country. What happens to women is not merely a "women's issue"; it is the central issue of stability, development, and durable peace. No nation can advance without women, and no enterprise that takes women off the table can come to much good.

12 THE US GOVERNMENT HAS NEVER SUPPORTED DEMOCRATIC ORGANIZATIONS

Elsa Rassbach interviews Zoya of
the Foreign Committee of RAWA

In June 2008 the Afghan activist Zoya of the Revolutionary Association of the Women of Afghanistan (RAWA) testified to the Human Rights Commission of the German Parliament (Bundestag) in an effort to persuade the German government to withdraw its troops from Afghanistan. At that time Elsa Rassbach, a US citizen living in Germany, interviewed Zoya in Berlin.

"Zoya" is a pseudonym. Despite more than seven years of US and NATO occupation and supposed democracy, the members of RAWA must still use pseudonyms to protect their organization, their families, and their work to liberate the women of Afghanistan. As a member of RAWA's Foreign Committee, Zoya has traveled to many countries, including the US and Spain as well as Germany. She received international acclaim with the 2003 publication of her dramatic autobiography, *Zoya's Story: An Afghan Woman's Battle for Freedom*, with John Follain and Rita Cristofari.

Rassbach: *What led you to decide to work with RAWA?*

Zoya: I'm from the generation of the war crimes in Afghanistan. I was born in 1979, and that was the year of the Soviet invasion. My generation has never enjoyed democracy, freedom, secularism, or peace in Afghanistan. After the withdrawal of the Soviets and the fall of the puppet regime, the darkest part of our history began when fundamentalists took power in 1992. That was the start of the odious part of our history, which continues until this day. Between 1992 and 1996, 80,000 civilians were killed in Kabul under the domination of the Northern Alliance, due to infight-ing between fundamentalist groups. They turned Kabul into a graveyard, where you could only see tears, fear, destruction, and blood. Then, when the Taliban came into power, they even raped seventy-year-olds and four-year-olds. The main reason I joined RAWA was the misery and pain of our people.

The US government has always played with the destiny of our poor people and has supported criminals, terrorists, and the worst enemies of our people. During the Cold War, the US created, nurtured, funded, and supported these groups against the Soviets. This spread misery and death in Afghanistan over the past three decades.

I was a war orphan; I lost my parents as the result of the war. I studied in RAWA's school, the Watan ("Homeland") School, in the refugee camp in Pakistan. They had a school for girls and one for boys. I was there through the sixth grade. I became aware of RAWA through the school. I found RAWA to be the most serious, honest, radical, anti-fundamen-talist, democratic organization fighting for justice and women's rights. I found it to give a voice to Afghan women who were not even regarded as human beings by the fundamentalist gangs. The suffering, destitution, and awful plight of my fellow countrywomen persuaded me to continue to fight against the brutal fundamentalists and for women's rights and democracy.

I began with RAWA at age fourteen. I am now twenty-eight and a member of the Foreign Committee. I'm in my third year of university, studying law.

Rassbach: *What is RAWA?*

Zoya: RAWA was first established in 1977 by Afghan intellectual women, headed by Meena, to fight for equality of men and women and against male chauvinism that was and is being practiced in our society. Most women were illiterate and took literacy courses and then decided to work with RAWA. Poor, uneducated women such as farmers' widows come to RAWA for help. We encourage them to fight for their rights and get political education.

In 1979 RAWA fought against the Russians and to expose the Russian puppet government through demonstrations, leaflets, and strikes. In 1987, RAWA's leader, Meena, was killed by agents of KHAD (Afghanistan branch of KGB) with direct help from the Islamic Party of Gulbuddin Hekmatyar. Our demonstrations were attacked, even in Pakistan. We had to live in a clandestine way. From 1992 to the present, we have fought any brand of Islamic fundamentalists, who are the main cause of our miseries and problems.

Now RAWA has hundreds of members as well as a large number of supporters, not only in Afghanistan, but all around the world. Being strongly against the fundamentalist warlords, the Taliban, and the puppet government of Hamid Karzai, we still can't work publicly in Afghanistan, and we continue to work semi-underground. In Afghanistan, we don't use the name RAWA for orphanages, literacy programs for women, handicraft centers for widows, or healthcare centers. The Afghan intelligence agency, which is run by warlords, follows us everywhere and creates problems for our members and supporters. Some of our supporters have been imprisoned and tortured simply for having copies of our magazine with them.

The US government has never supported democratic organizations like RAWA. Up until now, we have received not a penny from the US or any other government. At the same time, we have the honor of being supported by the peace-loving people of the US and other Western countries. We have received donations of $5 and even $1,000 for orphanages, schools, and political work. We are proud to rely on the small donations of our supporters and well-wishers in Afghanistan and abroad, which have a huge value for us. We have groups of dedicated supporters in many countries that really work hard to raise awareness and funds for RAWA projects.

Rassbach: *What is RAWA's position regarding the US and NATO troops in Afghanistan?*

Zoya: In 2001 the US and its allies occupied Afghanistan under the beautiful slogans of "war on terror," "women's rights," "liberation," and "democracy." But when they installed the brutal and criminal warlords after the fall of the Taliban, everyone knew that Afghanistan had once again become a chessboard for world powers. They have their long-term plans in Afghanistan, and the plight of our people, and especially of women, has been misused to legitimize the foreign military presence in our country.

The US invaded Afghanistan to fulfill its geopolitical, economic, and regional strategic interests and to transform Afghanistan into a strong military base in the region. In the past seven years, these troops have even further complicated the situation of Afghanistan. Not only have they pumped millions of dollars into the pockets of savage warlords, but the Taliban and other terrorist groups are more powerful today. They have turned Afghanistan into the opium capital of the world, and one of the reasons for invading Afghanistan was to get hold of this multi-billion-dollar drug business.

Afghan people have been badly betrayed by the US and NATO in the past few years. Despite billions in dollars of aid, Afghan people are living under awful conditions that are worse than they were under the Taliban's medieval rule. Afghanistan still faces a women's rights tragedy, and the everyday hardships of our masses are beyond imagination.

The US and NATO have imposed a corrupt mafia, a puppet government on the Afghan people, a government which is mostly comprised of warlords and drug lords. And now efforts are under way to share power with the Taliban and Islamic Party of Gulbuddin Hekmatyar.

The US and NATO are killing thousands of our innocent people, while at the same time their operations have no impact on the Taliban, because they are not really interested in peace and in stability in Afghanistan. The presence of the Taliban, al Qaeda, and other terrorist groups is in fact necessary for the US and NATO in order to have a reason for their permanent presence in Afghanistan. Everyone knows that the US, a superpower, together with the biggest military pact in the world, NATO, could in a matter of days, if not hours, defeat the Taliban and arrest Mullah Omar and Osama. But today they need such enemies to justify keeping their military machine in Afghanistan.

But even the foreign soldiers are the victims of the governments that send them to Afghanistan to be killed for nothing but guarding the profits of multinational corporations. These governments not only betray Afghans, but also their own citizens. They put in danger their own soldiers and spend taxpayers' money to push the region and the world toward more war and dangers. Here in Germany, I met a US veteran who had been in Afghanistan. I told him that it would be important to the whole world that he tell his story. He cried and said, "Because of you, I'll go and talk." Many former US veterans have shocking stories about how they witnessed that in the name of "liberation," these troops have been committing war crimes.

The troops should be withdrawn as soon as possible. This is the first step. They should adopt less bloody alternatives. We don't want their so-called liberation and democracy. If these troops do not withdraw, we are sure that the Afghan people will have no other option but to rise up against them. Our people are already deeply fed up with the situation. The jokes being made in Afghanistan are that the Taliban are getting the most from this situation.

Rassbach: *Would you not be afraid of a civil war if the US and NATO withdrew from Afghanistan?*

Zoya: RAWA supports the call for the withdrawal of the US and NATO troops because occupation is not a solution. They are constantly killing civilians, even at a wedding party. Do you think we are not human beings and don't have hearts? What would Americans do if an occupier were killing so many civilians in the US?

We have a good history in Afghanistan of throwing out occupiers, and this is a source of pride. But we have lost pride. Over forty countries have invaded us. People are frustrated, and they think the first step is to get the invaders out. Some may not agree with the Taliban, but some are paid to fight, and often they are starving; others are brainwashed, for example in the religious schools.

If there is a withdrawal, there will probably be a civil war between the Northern Alliance and the Taliban, but that would not be any worse than what is going on now. When these troops pull out at least we will then no more be an occupied country. It is the duty of Afghan people to get rid of the internal enemies, but today, our internal enemies are backed and supported by the external enemies that are the US and NATO.

The reason the fundamentalists are powerful is because they are always being supported by the US, which has given billions of dollars to the Northern Alliance, money that has gone into the pockets of warlords and drug lords. Today people are crying with hunger, selling their children for $5, but where did the billions go?

Rassbach: *What solutions would RAWA propose?*

Zoya: The withdrawal of military troops must be accompanied by other actions by governments, if they really want to help us as they claim. They must stop supporting any terrorist groups, including the Northern Alliance that destroyed Afghanistan before the Taliban came. There should also be sanctions on governments that support the Taliban, like Iran and Pakistan. Warlords should be brought to the International Court for crimes against humanity.

If they really have genuine concern for Afghanistan and want peace and stability in the country, the solution would be to support the democratic-minded organizations and individuals in Afghanistan, but in the past few years, much pressure has been put on such groups to give up. Today the democratic organizations are weak because no one helps them. If they received support, they would grow strong. And the democratic forces need to unite and fight against the fundamentalists.

The message of RAWA to freedom-loving people is to support the democratic organizations of Afghanistan. Freedom, democracy, and justice cannot be enforced at gunpoint by a foreign country; they are the values that can be achieved only by our people and democracy-loving forces through a hard, decisive, and long struggle. Those who claim to donate these values to the Afghan people through force will only push our country into slavery. It is our responsibility to stand up to fundamentalists and occupations.

Part III FACTS ON THE GROUND

13 GOING FOR BROKE:
SIX WAYS THE AF-PAK WAR IS EXPANDING

By Tom Engelhardt

Yes, Stanley McChrystal is the general from the dark side (and proud of it). So the recent sacking of Afghan commander General David McKiernan after less than a year in the field and McChrystal's appointment as the man to run the Afghan War seems to signal that the Obama administration is going for broke. It's heading straight into what, in the Vietnam era, was known as "the big muddy."

General McChrystal comes from a world where killing by any means is the norm and a blanket of secrecy provides the necessary protection. For five years he commanded the Pentagon's super-secret Joint Special Operations Command (JSOC), which, among other things, ran what Seymour Hersh has described as an "executive assassination wing" out of Vice President Cheney's office. (Cheney just returned the favor by giving the newly appointed general a ringing endorsement: "I think you'd be hard put to find anyone better than Stan McChrystal.")

McChrystal gained a certain renown when President Bush outed him as the man responsible for tracking down and eliminating al-Qaeda-in-Mesopotamia leader Abu Musab al-Zarqawi. The secret force of "manhunters" he commanded had its own secret detention and interrogation center near Baghdad, Camp Nama, where bad things happened regularly, and the unit there, Task Force 6-26, had its own slogan: "If you don't make them bleed, they can't prosecute for it." Since some of the task force's men were, in the end, prosecuted, the bleeding evidently wasn't avoided.

In the Bush years, McChrystal was reputedly extremely close to Secretary of Defense Donald Rumsfeld. The super-secret force he commanded was, in fact, part of Rumsfeld's effort to seize control of, and Pentagonize, the covert, on-the-ground activities that were once the purview of the CIA.

Behind McChrystal lies a string of targeted executions that may run into the hundreds, as well as accusations of torture and abuse by troops under his command (and a role in the cover-up of the circumstances surrounding the death of Army Ranger and former National Football League player Pat Tillman). The general has reportedly long thought of Afghanistan and Pakistan as a single battlefield, which means that he was a premature adherent to the idea of an Af-Pak—that is, expanded—war. While in Afghanistan in 2008, the *New York Times* reported, he was a "key advocate . . . of a plan, ultimately approved by President George W. Bush, to use American commandos to strike at Taliban sanctuaries in Pakistan." This end-of-term Bush program provoked such anger and blowback in Pakistan that it was reportedly halted after two cross-border raids, one of which killed civilians.

All of this offers more than a hint of the sort of "new thinking and new approaches"—to use Secretary of Defense Robert Gates's words—that the Obama administration expects General McChrystal to bring to the devolving Af-Pak battlefield. He is, in a sense, both a legacy figure from the worst days of the Bush-Cheney-Rumsfeld era and the first-born child of Obama-era Washington's growing desperation and hysteria over the wars it inherited.

HAGIOGRAPHY

And here's the good news: we luv the guy. Just luv him to death.

We loved him back in 2006, when Bush first outed him and *Newsweek* reporters Michael Hirsh and John Barry dubbed him "a rising star" in the Army and one of the "Jedi Knights who are fighting in what Cheney calls 'the shadows.'"

It's no different today in what's left of the mainstream news analysis business. In that mix of sports lingo, Hollywood-ese, and plain hyperbole that makes armchair war strategizing just so darn much fun, *Washington Post* columnist David Ignatius, for instance, claimed that Centcom commander General David Petraeus, who picked McChrystal as his man in Afghanistan, is "assembling an all-star team" and that McChrystal himself is "a rising superstar who, like Petraeus, has helped reinvent the US Army." Is that all?

When it came to pure, instant hagiography, however, the prize went to Elisabeth Bumiller and Mark Mazzetti of the *New York Times*, who wrote a front-pager, "A General Steps from the Shadows," that painted a picture of McChrystal as a mutant cross between Superman and a saint.

Among other things, it described the general as "an ascetic who . . . usually eats just one meal a day, in the evening, to avoid sluggishness. He is known for operating on a few hours' sleep and for running to and from work while listening to audio books on an iPod . . . [He has] an encyclopedic, even obsessive, knowledge about the lives of terrorists . . . [He is] a warrior-scholar, comfortable with diplomats, politicians . . ." and so on. The quotes Bumiller and Mazzetti dug up from others were no less spectacular: "He's got all the Special Ops attributes, plus an intellect." "If you asked me the first thing that comes to mind about General McChrystal . . . I think of no body fat."

From the gush of good cheer about his appointment, you might almost conclude that the general was not human at all, but an advanced android (a good one, of course!) and the "elite" world (of murder and abuse) he emerged from an unbearably sexy one.

Above all, as we're told here and elsewhere, what's so *good* about the new appointment is that General McChrystal is "more aggressive" than his stick-in-the-mud predecessor. He will, as Bumiller and Thom Shanker report in another piece, bring "a more aggressive and innovative approach to a worsening seven-year war." The general, we're assured, likes operations without body fat, but with plenty of punch. And though no one quite says this, given his closeness to Rumsfeld and possibly Cheney, both desperately eager to "take the gloves off" on a planetary scale, his mentality is undoubtedly a global-war-on-terror one, which translates into no respect for boundaries, restraints, or the sovereignty of others. After all, as journalist Gareth Porter pointed out recently in a thoughtful *Asia Times* portrait of the new Afghan War commander, Secretary of Defense Donald Rumsfeld granted the parent of JSOC, the Special Operations Command (SOCOM), "the authority to carry out actions unilaterally anywhere on the globe."

Think of McChrystal's appointment, then, as a decision in Washington to dispatch the bull directly to the china shop with the most meager of hopes that the results won't be smashed Afghans and Pakistanis. The *Post's* Ignatius even compares McChrystal's boss Petraeus and Obama's special envoy to the region, Richard Holbrooke, to "two headstrong bulls in a small paddock." He then concludes his paean to all of them with this passage— far more ominous than he means it to be: "Obama knows the immense difficulty of trying to fix a broken Afghanistan and make it a functioning, modern country. But with his two bulls, Petraeus and Holbrooke, he's marching his presidency into the 'graveyard of empires' anyway."

McChrystal is evidently the third bull, the one slated to start knocking over the tombstones.

AN EXPANDING AF-PAK WAR

Of course, there are now so many bulls in this particular china shop that smashing is increasingly the name of the game. At this point, the early moves of the Obama administration, when combined with the momentum of the situation it inherited, have resulted in the expansion of the Af-Pak War in at least six areas, which only presage further expansion in the months to come:

1. *Expanding Troop Commitment*: In February 2009 President Obama ordered a "surge" of 17,000 extra troops into Afghanistan, increasing US forces there by 50 percent. (Then-commander McKiernan had called for 30,000 new troops.) In March, another 4,000 American military advisers and trainers were promised. The first of the surge troops, reportedly ill-equipped, are already arriving. In March, it was announced that this troop surge would be accompanied by a "civilian surge" of diplomats, advisers, and the like; in April, it was reported that, because the requisite diplomats and advisers couldn't be found, the civilian surge would actually be made up largely of military personnel.

In preparation for this influx, there has been massive base and outpost building in the southern parts of the country, including the construction of 443-acre Camp Leatherneck in that region's "desert of death." When finished, it will support up to 8,000 US troops, and a raft of helicopters and planes. Its airfield, which is under construction, has been described as the "largest such project in the world in a combat setting."

2. *Expanding CIA Drone War*: The CIA is running an escalating secret drone war in the skies over the Pakistani borderlands with Afghanistan, a

"targeted" assassination program of the sort that McChrystal specialized in while in Iraq. Since September 2008, more than three dozen drone attacks—the *Los Angeles Times* put the number at fifty-five—have been launched, as opposed to ten in 2006–2007. The program has reportedly taken out a number of mid-level al Qaeda and Taliban leaders, but also caused significant civilian casualties, destabilized the Pashtun border areas of Pakistan, and fostered support for the Islamic guerrillas in those regions. As Noah Shachtman wrote in May 2009 at his Danger Room website:

> According to the American press, a pair of missiles from the unmanned aircraft killed "at least twenty-five militants." In the local media, the dead were simply described as "twenty-nine tribesmen present there." That simple difference in description underlies a serious problem in the campaign against the Taliban and Al Qaeda. To Americans, the drones over Pakistan are terrorist-killers. In Pakistan, the robotic planes are wiping out neighbors.

David Kilcullen, a key advisor to Petraeus during the Iraq "surge" months, and counterinsurgency expert Andrew McDonald Exum called for a moratorium on these attacks on the *New York Times* op-ed page. ("Press reports suggest that over the last three years drone strikes have killed about fourteen terrorist leaders. But, according to Pakistani sources, they have also killed some 700 civilians. This is fifty civilians for every militant killed, a hit rate of 2 percent—hardly 'precision.'") As it happens, however, the Obama administration is deeply committed to its drone war. As CIA Director Leon Panetta put the matter, "Very frankly, it's the only game in town in terms of confronting or trying to disrupt the al Qaeda leadership."

3. *Expanding Air Force Drone War*: The US Air Force now seems to be getting into the act as well. There are conflicting reports about just what it is trying to do, but it has evidently brought its own set of Predator and Reaper drones into play in Pakistani skies, in conjunction, it seems, with a somewhat reluctant Pakistani military. Though the outlines of this program are foggy at best, it nonetheless represents an expansion of the war.

4. *Expanding Political Interference*: Quite a different kind of escalation is also under way. Washington is evidently attempting to insert yet another figure

from the Bush-Cheney-Rumsfeld era into the Afghan mix. Not so long ago, Zalmay Khalilzad, the neocon former American viceroy in Kabul and then Baghdad, was considering making a run for the Afghan presidency against Hamid Karzai, the leader the Obama administration is desperate to ditch. In March 2009, reports—hotly denied by Holbrooke and others—broke in the British press of a US/British plan to "undermine President Karzai of Afghanistan by forcing him to install a powerful chief of staff to run the Government." Karzai, so the rumors went, would be reduced to "figure-head" status, while a "chief executive with prime ministerial-style powers" not provided for in the Afghan Constitution would essentially take over the running of the weak and corrupt government.

On May 21, 2009, Helene Cooper reported on the front page of the *New York Times* that Khalilzad would be that man. He "could assume a power-ful, unelected position inside the Afghan government under a plan he is discussing with Hamid Karzai, the Afghan president, according to senior American and Afghan officials." He would then be "the chief executive officer of Afghanistan."

Cooper's report was filled with official denials that these negotiations involved Washington in any way. Yet if they succeeded, an American citi-zen, a former US Ambassador to the UN as well as to Kabul, would end up functionally atop the Karzai government just as the Obama administration was eagerly pursuing a stepped-up war against the Taliban.

Why officials in Washington imagine that Afghans might actually accept such a figure was the mystery of the moment. It's best to think of this plan as the kinder, gentler, soft-power version of the Kennedy administration's 1963 decision to sign off on the coup that led to the assassination of South Vietnamese autocrat Ngo Dinh Diem. Then, too, top Washington officials were distressed that a puppet who seemed to be losing support was, like Karzai, also acting in an increasingly independent manner when it came to playing his appointed role in an American drama. That assassination, by the way, only increased instability in South Vietnam, leading to a succession of weak military regimes and paving the way for a further unraveling there. This American expansion of the war would likely have similar consequences.

5. Expanding War in Pakistan: Meanwhile, in Pakistan itself, mayhem has ensued, again in significant part thanks to Washington, whose disastrous

Afghan War and escalating drone attacks have helped to destabilize the Pashtun regions of the country. At time of writing (May, 2009), the Pakistani military—pushed and threatened by Washington (with the loss of military aid, among other things)—has smashed full force into the districts of Buner and Swat, which had, in recent months, been largely taken over by the Islamic fundamentalist guerrillas we call "the Pakistani Taliban."

It's been a massive show of force by a military configured for smash-mouth war with India, not urban or village warfare with lightly armed guerrillas. The Pakistani military has loosed its jets, helicopter gunships, and artillery on the region (even as the CIA drone strikes continue), killing unknown numbers of civilians and, far more significantly, causing a massive exodus of the local population. In some areas, well more than half the population has fled Taliban depredations and indiscriminate fire from the military. Those that remain in besieged towns and cities, often without electricity, with the dead in the streets, and fast disappearing supplies of food, are clearly in trouble.

With nearly 1.5 million Pakistanis turned into refugees just since the latest offensive began, UN officials are suggesting that this could be the worst refugee crisis since the Rwandan genocide in 1994. Talk about the destabilization of a country.

In the long run, this may only increase the anger of Pashtuns in the tribal areas of Pakistan at both the Americans and the Pakistani military and government. The rise of Pashtun nationalism and a fight for an "Islamic Pashtunistan" would prove a dangerous development indeed. This latest offensive is what Washington thought it wanted, but undoubtedly the old saw, "Be careful what you wish for, lest it come true," applies. Already a panicky Washington is planning to rush $110 million in refugee assistance to the country.

6. Expanding Civilian Death Toll and Blowback: As Taliban attacks in Afghanistan rise and that loose guerrilla force (more like a coalition of various Islamist, tribal, warlord, and criminal groups) spreads into new areas, the American air war in Afghanistan continues to take a heavy toll on Afghan civilians, while manufacturing ever more enemies as well as deep resentment and protest in that country. One such incident, possibly the worst since the Taliban was defeated in 2001, involves the deaths of up to 147 Afghans in the Bala Baluk district of Farah Province, according to accounts that have come out of the villages attacked. Up to ninety-five of the dead were under eighteen, one Afghan lawmaker involved in investigating the incident claims, and up to sixty-five of them women or girls. These deaths came after Americans were called into an escalating fight between the Taliban and Afghan police and military units, and, in turn, called in devastating air strikes by two US jets and a B-1 bomber (which, villagers claim, hit them after the Taliban fighters had left).

Despite American pledges to own up to and apologize more quickly for civilian deaths, the post-carnage events followed a predictable stonewalling pattern, including a begrudging step-by-step retreat in the face of independent claims and reports. The Americans first denied that anything much had happened; then claimed that they had killed mainly Taliban "militants"; then that the Taliban had themselves used grenades to kill most of the civilians (a charge later partially withdrawn as "thinly sourced"); and finally, that the numbers of Afghan dead were "extremely over-exaggerated," and that the urge for payment from the Afghan government might be partially responsible.

An investigation, as always, was launched that never seems to end, while the Americans wait for the story to fade from view. As of this moment, in May 2009, while still awaiting the results of a "very exhaustive" investigation, American spokesmen nonetheless claim that only twenty to thirty civilians died along with up to sixty-five Taliban insurgents. In these years, however, the record tells us that, when weighing the stories offered by surviving villagers and those of American officials, believe the villagers. Put more bluntly, in such situations, we lie, they die.

Two things make this "incident" at Bala Baluk more striking. First of all, according to Jerome Starkey of the British *Independent*, another Rumsfeld creation, the US Marine Corps Forces Special Operations Command (MarSOC), the Marines' version of JSOC, was centrally involved, as it had been in two other major civilian slaughters, one near Jalalabad in 2007 (committed by a MarSOC unit that dubbed itself "Taskforce Violence"), the second in 2008 at the village of Azizabad in Herat Province. McChrystal's appointment, reports Starkey, "prompted speculation that [similar] commando counterinsurgency missions will increase in the battle to beat the Taliban."

Second, back in Washington, National Security Adviser James Jones and head of the Joint Chiefs Admiral Mike Mullen, fretting about civilian casualties in Afghanistan and faced with President Karzai's repeated pleas to cease air attacks on Afghan villages, nonetheless refused to consider the possibility. Both, in fact, used the same image. As Jones told ABC's George Stephanopoulos: "Well, I think he understands that . . . we have to have the full complement of . . . our offensive military power when we need it . . . We can't fight with one hand tied behind our back . . ."

In a world in which the US is the military equivalent of the multi-armed Hindu god Shiva, this is one of the truly strange, if long-lasting, American images. It was, for instance, used by President George H. W. Bush on the eve of the first Gulf War. "No hands," he said, "are going to be tied behind backs. This is not a Vietnam."

Forgetting the levels of firepower loosed in Vietnam, the image itself is abidingly odd. After all, in everyday speech, the challenge "I could beat you with one hand tied behind my back" is a bravado offer of voluntary restraint and an implicit admission that fighting any other way would make one a bully. So hidden in the image, both when the elder Bush used it and today, is a most un-American acceptance of the United States as a bully nation, about to be restrained by no one, least of all itself.

Apologize or stonewall, one thing remains certain: the air war will continue and so civilians will continue to die. The idea that the US might actually be better off with one "hand" tied behind its back is now so alien to us as to be beyond serious consideration.

THE PRESSURE OF AN EXPANDING WAR

President Obama has opted for a down-and-dirty war strategy in search of some at least minimalist form of success. For this, McChrystal is the poster boy. Former Afghan commander General McKiernan believed that, "as a NATO commander, my mandate stops at the [Afghan] border. So unless there is a clear case of self-protection to fire across the border, we don't consider any operations across the border in the tribal areas."

That the "responsibilities" of US generals fighting the Afghan War "ended at the border with Pakistan," Mark Mazzetti and Eric Schmitt of the *Times* report, is now considered part of an "old mind-set." McChrystal represents those "fresh eyes" that Secretary of Defense Robert Gates talked about in the press conference announcing the general's appointment. As Mazzetti and Schmitt point out, "Among [McChrystal's] last projects as the head of the Joint Special Operations Command was to better coordinate Pentagon and Central Intelligence Agency efforts on both sides of the porous border."

For those old enough to remember, we've been here before. Administrations that start down a path of expansion in such a war find themselves strangely locked in—psychically, if nothing else—if things don't work out as expected and the situation continues to deteriorate. In Vietnam, the result was escalation without end. President Obama and his foreign policy team now seem locked into an expanding war. Despite the fact that the application of force has not only failed for years, but actually fed that expansion, they also seem to be locked into a policy of applying ever greater force, with the goal of, as the *Post*'s Ignatius puts it, cracking the "Taliban coalition" and bringing elements of it to the bargaining table.

So keep an eye out for whatever goes wrong, as it most certainly will, and then for the pressures on Washington to respond with further expansions of what is already "Obama's war." With McChrystal in charge in Afghanistan, for instance, it seems reasonable to assume that the urge to sanction new special forces raids into Pakistan will grow. After all, frustration in Washington is already building, for however much the Pakistani military may be taking on the Taliban in Swat or Buner, don't expect its military or civilian leaders to be terribly interested in what happens near the Afghan border.

As Tony Karon of the Rootless Cosmopolitan blog puts the matter: "The current military campaign is designed to enforce a limit on the Taliban's reach within Pakistan, confining it to the movement's heartland." And that heartland is the Afghan border region. For one thing, the Pakistani military (and the country's intelligence services, which essentially brought the Taliban into being long ago) are focused on India. They want a Pashtun ally across the border, Taliban or otherwise, where they fear the Indians are making inroads.

So the frustration of a war in which the enemy has no borders and we do is bound to rise along with the fighting, long predicted to intensify this year. We now have a more aggressive "team" in place. Soon enough, if the fighting in the Afghan south and along the Pakistani border doesn't go as planned, pressure for the president to send in those other 10,000 troops

General McKiernan asked for may rise as well, as could pressure to apply more air power, more drone power, more of almost anything. And yet, as former CIA station chief in Kabul, Graham Fuller, wrote recently, in the region "crises have only grown worse under the US military footprint."

And what if, as the war continues its slow arc of expansion, the "Washington coalition" is the one that cracks first? What then?

14 THE SHADOW WAR: MAKING SENSE OF THE NEW CIA BATTLEFIELD

By Tom Engelhardt and Nick Turse

It was a Christmas and New Year's from hell for American intelligence, that $75 billion labyrinth of at least sixteen major agencies and a handful of minor ones. As the old year was preparing to be rung out, so were our intelligence agencies, which managed not to connect every obvious clue to a (literally) seat-of-the-pants al Qaeda operation. It hardly mattered that the underwear bomber's case—except for the placement of the bomb material—almost exactly, even outrageously, replicated the infamous, and equally inept, "shoe bomber" plot of eight years ago.

That would have been bad enough, but the New Year brought worse. Army Major General Michael Flynn, US and NATO forces deputy chief of staff for intelligence in Afghanistan, released a report in which he labeled military intelligence in the war zone—but by implication US intelligence operatives generally—"clueless." They were, he wrote, "ignorant of local economics and landowners, hazy about who the powerbrokers are and how they might be influenced . . . and disengaged from people in the best position to find answers . . . Eight years into the war in Afghanistan, the US intelligence community is only marginally relevant to the overall strategy."

As if to prove the general's point, Humam Khalil Abu-Mulal al-Balawi, a Jordanian doctor with a penchant for writing inspirational essays on jihadi websites and an "unproven asset" for the CIA, somehow entered a key Agency forward operating base in Afghanistan unsearched, supposedly with information on al Qaeda's leadership so crucial that a high-level CIA team was assembled to hear it and Washington was alerted. He proved to be either a double or a triple agent and killed seven CIA operatives, one of whom was the base chief, by detonating a suicide vest bomb, while wounding yet more, including the Agency's number-two operative in the country. The first suicide bomber to penetrate a US base in Afghanistan, he blew a hole in the CIA's relatively small cadre of agents knowledgeable on al Qaeda and the Taliban.

It was an intelligence disaster splayed all over the headlines: "Taliban bomber wrecks CIA's shadowy war," "Killings Rock Afghan Strategy," "Suicide bomber who attacked CIA post was trusted informant from Jordan." It seemed to sum up the hapless nature of America's intelligence operations as the CIA, with all the latest technology and every imaginable resource on hand, including the latest in Hellfire missile-armed drone aircraft, was out-thought and out-maneuvered by low-tech enemies.

No one could say that the deaths and the blow to the American war effort weren't well covered. There were major TV reports night after night and scores of news stories, many given front-page treatment. And yet lurking behind those deaths and the man who caused them lay a bigger American war story that went largely untold. It was a tale of a new-style battlefield that the American public knows remarkably little about, and that bears little relationship to the Afghan War as we imagine it or as our leaders generally discuss it.

We don't even have a language to describe it accurately. Think of it as a battlefield filled with muscled-up, militarized intelligence operatives, hired-gun contractors doing military duty, and privatized "native" guard forces. Add in robot assassins in the air 24/7 and kick-down-the-door-style night-time "intelligence" raids, "surges" you didn't know were happening, strings of military bases you had no idea were out there, and secretive international collaborations you were unaware the US was involved in. In Afghanistan, the American military is only part of the story. There's also a polyglot "army" representing the US that wears no uniforms and fights shape-shifting enemies to the death in a murderous war of multiple assassinations and civilian slaughter, all enveloped in a blanket of secrecy.

BLACK OPS AND BLACK SITES

Secrecy is, of course, a part of war. The surprise attack is only a surprise if secrecy is maintained. In wartime, crucial information must be kept from an enemy capable of using it. But what if, as in our case, wartime never ends, while secrecy becomes endemic, as well as profitable and privatizable, and much of the information available to both sides on our shadowy new battlefield is mainly being kept from the American people? The coverage of the suicide attack on Forward Operating Base (FOB) Chapman offered a rare, very partial window into that strange war—but only if you were willing to read piles of news reports looking for tiny bits of information that could be pieced together.

We did just that and here's what we found. Let's start with FOB Chapman, where the suicide bombing took place. An old Soviet base near the Pakistani border, it was renamed after a Green Beret who fought beside CIA agents and was the first American to die in the invasion of Afghanistan in 2001. It sits in isolation near the town of Khost, just miles from the larger Camp Salerno, a forward operating base used mainly by US Special Operations troops. Occupied by the CIA since 2001, Chapman is regularly described as "small" or "tiny" and, in one report, as having "a forbidding network of barriers, barbed wire and watchtowers." Though a State Department provisional reconstruction team has been stationed there (as well as personnel from the US Agency for International Development and the US Department of Agriculture), and though it "was officially a camp for civilians involved in reconstruction," FOB Chapman is "well-known locally as a CIA base"—an "open secret," as another report put it.

The base is guarded by Afghan irregulars, sometimes referred to in news reports as "Afghan contractors," about whom we know next to nothing. ("CIA officials on Thursday would not discuss what guard service they had at the base.") Despite the recent suicide bombing, according to Julian Barnes and Greg Miller of the *Los Angeles Times*, a "program to hire Afghans to guard US forward operating bases would not be canceled. Under that program, which is beginning in eastern Afghanistan, Afghans will guard towers, patrol perimeter fences and man checkpoints." Also on FOB Chapman were employees of the private security contractor Xe (formerly Blackwater) which has had a close relationship with the CIA in Afghanistan. We know this because of reports that two of the dead "CIA" agents were Xe operatives.

Someone else of interest was at FOB Chapman and so at that fateful meeting with the Jordanian doctor al-Balawi—Sharif Ali bin Zeid, a captain in the Jordanian intelligence service, the eighth person killed in the blast. It turns out that al-Balawi was an agent of Jordanian intelligence, which held (and abused) torture suspects kidnapped and disappeared by the CIA in the years of George W. Bush's Global War on Terror. The service reportedly continues to work closely with the Agency, and the captain was evidently running al-Balawi. That's what we now know about the polyglot group at FOB Chapman on the front lines of the Agency's black-ops war against al Qaeda, the Taliban, and the allied fighters of the Haqqani network in nearby Pakistan. If there were other participants, they weren't among the bodies.

THE AGENCY SURGES

And here's something that's far clearer in the wake of the bombing: among our vast network of bases in Afghanistan, the CIA has its own designated bases—as, by the way, do US Special Operations forces, and according to *Nation* reporter Jeremy Scahill, even private contractor Xe. Without better reporting on the subject, it's hard to get a picture of these bases, but Siobhan Gorman of the *Wall Street Journal* tells us that a typical CIA base houses no more than fifteen to twenty Agency operatives (which means that al-Balawi's explosion killed or wounded more than half of the team on FOB Chapman).

And don't imagine that we're only talking about a base or two. In the single most substantive post-blast report on the CIA, Mark Mazzetti of the *New York Times* wrote that the Agency has "an archipelago of firebases in southern and eastern Afghanistan," most built in the last year. An *archipelago*? Imagine that. And it's also reported that even more of them are in the works.

With this goes another bit of information that the *Wall Street Journal* seems to have been the first to drop into its reports. While you've heard about President Obama's surge in American troops and possibly even State Department personnel in Afghanistan, you've undoubtedly heard little or nothing about a CIA surge in the region, and yet the *Journal*'s reporters tell us that Agency personnel will increase by 20–25 percent in the surge months. By the time the CIA is fully bulked up with all its agents, paramilitaries, and private contractors in place, Afghanistan will represent, according to Julian Barnes of the *Los Angeles Times*, one of the largest "stations" in Agency history.

This, in turn, implies other surges. There will be a surge in base-building to house those agents, and a surge in "native" guards—at least until another suicide bomber hits a base thanks to Taliban supporters among them or one of them turns a weapon on the occupants of a base—and undoubtedly a surge in Blackwater-style mercenaries as well. Keep in mind that, as January 2009 the latest figure on private contractors suggests that 56,000 more of them will surge into Afghanistan in the period from January of this year to summer 2011, far more than surging US troops, State Department employees, and CIA operatives combined. And don't forget the thousands of non-CIA "uniformed and civilian intelligence personnel serving with the Defense Department and joint interagency operations in the country," who will undoubtedly surge as well.

MAKING WAR

The efforts of the CIA operatives at Forward Operating Base Chapman were reportedly focused on "collecting information about militant networks in Afghanistan and Pakistan and plotting missions to kill the networks' top leaders," especially those in the Haqqani network in North Waziristan just across the Pakistani border. They were evidently running "informants" into Pakistan to find targets for the Agency's ongoing drone assassination war. These drone attacks in Pakistan have themselves been on an unparalleled surge course ever since Barack Obama entered office; forty-four to fifty (or more) have been launched in the last year, with civilian casualties running into the hundreds. Like local Pashtuns, the Agency essentially doesn't recognize a border. For them, the Afghan and Pakistani tribal borderlands are a single world.

In this way, as Paul Woodward of the website War in Context has pointed out, "Two groups of combatants, neither of whom wear uniforms, are slugging it out on the Afghan-Pakistan border. Each group has identified what it regards as high-value targets and each is using its own available means to hit these targets. The Taliban/Qaeda are using suicide bombers while the CIA is using Hellfire missiles."

Since the devastating explosion at FOB Chapman, statements of vengeance have been coming out of CIA mouths—of a kind that, when offered by the Taliban or al Qaeda, we consider typical of a backward, "tribal" society. In any case, the secret war is evidently becoming a private and personal one. Dr. al-Balawi's suicide attack essentially took out a major part of the Agency's targeting information system. As one unnamed NATO official told the *New York Times*, "These were not people who wrote things down in the computer or in notebooks. It was all in their heads . . . [The CIA is] pulling in new people from all over the world, but how long will it take to rebuild the networks, to get up to speed? Lots of it is irrecoverable." And the Agency was already generally known to be "desperately short of personnel who speak the language or are knowledgeable about the region." Nonetheless, drone attacks have suddenly escalated—at least five in the week after the suicide bombing, all evidently aimed at "an area believed to be a hideout for militants involved." These sound like vengeance attacks and are likely to be particularly counterproductive.

To sum up, US intelligence agents, having lost out to enemy "intelligence agents," even after being transformed into full-time assassins, are now locked in a mortal struggle with an enemy for whom assassination is also a crucial tactic, but whose operatives seem to have better informants and better information.

In this war, drones are not the Agency's only weapon. The CIA also seems to specialize in running highly controversial, kick-down-the-door "night raids" in conjunction with Afghan paramilitary forces. Such raids, when launched by US Special Operations forces, have led to highly publicized and heavily protested civilian casualties. Sometimes, according to reports, the CIA actually conducts them in conjunction with Special Operations forces. In a recent American-led night raid in Kunar Province, eight young students were, according to Afghan sources, detained, handcuffed, and executed. The leadership of this raid has been attributed, euphemistically, to "other government agencies" (OGAs) or "non-military Americans." These raids, whether successful in the limited sense or not, don't fit comfortably with the Obama administration's "hearts and minds" counterinsurgency strategy.

THE MILITARIZATION OF THE AGENCY

As the identities of some of the fallen CIA operatives at FOB Chapman became known, a pattern began to emerge. There was thirty-seven-year-old Harold Brown, Jr., who formerly served in the Army. There was Scott Roberson, a former Navy SEAL, who did several tours of duty in Iraq, where he provided protection to officials considered at high risk. There was Jeremy Wise, thirty-five, an ex-Navy SEAL who left the military last year, signed up with Xe, and ended up working for the CIA. Similarly, forty-six-year-old Dane Paresi, a retired Special Forces master sergeant turned Xe hired gun, also died in the blast.

For years, Chalmers Johnson, himself a former CIA consultant, has referred to the Agency as "the president's private army." Today, that moniker seems truer than ever. While the civilian CIA has always had a paramilitary component, known as the Special Activities Division, the unit was generally relatively small and dormant. Instead, military personnel like the Army's Special Forces or indigenous troops carried out the majority of the CIA's combat missions. After the 9/11 attacks, however, President Bush empowered the Agency to hunt down, kidnap, and assassinate suspected al Qaeda operatives, and the CIA's traditional specialties of spycraft and intelligence analysis took a distinct backseat to Special Activities Division operations, as its agents set up a global gulag of ghost prisons, conducted interrogations-by-torture, and then added those missile-armed drone and assassination programs.

The military backgrounds of the fallen CIA operatives cast a light on the way the world of "intelligence" is increasingly muscling up and becoming militarized. This past summer, when a former CIA official suggested the Agency might be backing away from risky programs, a current official spat back from the shadows: "If anyone thinks the CIA has gotten risk-averse recently, go ask al Qaeda and the Taliban ... The Agency's still doing cutting-edge stuff in all kinds of dangerous places." At around the same time, reports were emerging that Blackwater/Xe was providing security, arming drones, and "perform[ing] some of the Agency's most important assignments" at secret bases in Pakistan and Afghanistan. It also emerged that the CIA had paid contractors from Blackwater to take part in a covert assassination program in Afghanistan.

Add this all together and you have the grim face of "intelligence" at war in 2010—a new micro-brew when it comes to Washington's conflicts. Today, in Afghanistan, a militarized mix of CIA operatives and ex-military mercenaries as well as native recruits and robot aircraft is fighting a war "in the shadows" (as they used to say in the Cold War era). This is no longer "intelligence" as anyone imagines it, nor is it "military" as military was once defined, not when US operations have gone mercenary and native in such a big way. This is pure "lord of the flies" stuff—beyond oversight, beyond any law, including the laws of war. And worse yet, from all available evidence, despite claims that the drone war is knocking off mid-level enemies, it seems remarkably ineffective. All it may be doing is spreading the war farther and digging it in deeper.

Talk about "counterinsurgency" as much as you want, but this is another kind of battlefield, and "protecting the people" plays no part in it. And, of course, this is only what can be gleaned from afar about a semi-secret war that is being poorly reported. Who knows what it costs when you include the US hired guns, the Afghan contractors, the bases, the drones, and the rest of the personnel and infrastructure? Nor do we know what else, or who else, is involved, and what else is being done. Clearly, however, all those billions of "intelligence" dollars are going into the blackest of black holes.

15 THE 700 MILITARY BASES OF AFGHANISTAN: BLACK SITES IN THE EMPIRE OF BASES

By Nick Turse

In the nineteenth century, it was a fort used by British forces. In the twentieth century, Soviet troops moved into the crumbling facilities. In December 2009, at this site in the Shinwar district of Afghanistan's Nangarhar Province, US troops joined members of the Afghan National Army in preparing the way for the next round of foreign occupation. On its grounds, a new military base is expected to rise, one of hundreds of camps and outposts scattered across the country.

Nearly a decade after the Bush administration launched its invasion of Afghanistan, TomDispatch website offers the first actual count of American, NATO, and other coalition bases there, as well as facilities used by the Afghan security forces. Such bases range from relatively small sites like Shinwar to mega-bases that resemble small American towns. Today, according to official sources, approximately 700 bases of every size dot the Afghan countryside, and more, like the one in Shinwar, are under construction or soon will be as part of a base-building boom that began last year.

Existing in the shadows, rarely reported on and little talked about, this base-building program is nonetheless staggering in size and scope, and heavily dependent on supplies imported from abroad, which means that it is also extraordinarily expensive. It has added significantly to the already long secret list of Pentagon property overseas and raises questions about just how long, after the planned beginning of a drawdown of American forces in 2011, the US will still be garrisoning Afghanistan.

400 FOREIGN BASES IN AFGHANISTAN

According to Colonel Wayne Shanks, a spokesman for the US-led International Security Assistance Force (ISAF), there are, at present, nearly 400 US and coalition bases in Afghanistan, including camps, forward operating bases, and combat outposts. In addition, there are at least 300 Afghan National Army (ANA) and Afghan National Police (ANP) bases, most of them built, maintained, or supported by the US. A small number of the coalition sites are mega-bases like Kandahar Airfield, which boasts one of the busiest runways in the world, and Bagram Air Base, a former Soviet facility that received a makeover, complete with Burger King and Popeyes outlets, and now serves more than 20,000 US troops, in addition to thousands of coalition forces and civilian contractors.

In fact, Kandahar, which housed 9,000 coalition troops as recently as 2007, is expected to have a population of as many as 35,000 troops by the time President Obama's surge is complete, according to Colonel Kevin Wilson who oversees building efforts in the southern half of Afghanistan for the US Army Corps of Engineers. On the other hand, the Shinwar site, according to Sergeant Tracy J. Smith of the US 48th Infantry Brigade Combat Team, will be a small forward operating base (FOB) that will host both Afghan troops and foreign forces.

Last fall, it was reported that more than $200 million in construction projects—from barracks to cargo storage facilities—were planned for or in progress at Bagram. Substantial construction funds have also been set aside by the US Air Force to upgrade its air power capacity at Kandahar. For example, $65 million has been allocated to build additional apron space (where aircraft can be parked, serviced, and loaded or unloaded) to accommodate more close-air support for soldiers in the field and a greater intelligence, surveillance, and reconnaissance capability. Another $61 million has also been earmarked for the construction of a cargo helicopter apron and a tactical airlift apron there.

Kandahar is just one of many sites currently being upgraded. Exact figures on the number of facilities being enlarged, improved, or hardened are unavailable but, according a spokesman for ISAF, the military plans to expand several more bases to accommodate the increase of troops as part of Afghan War commander Stanley McChrystal's surge strategy. In addition, at least twelve more bases are slated to be built to help handle the 30,000 extra American troops and thousands of NATO forces beginning to arrive in the country.

"Currently we have over \$3 billion worth of work going on in Afghanistan," says Colonel Wilson, "and probably by the summer, when the dust settles from all the uplift, we'll have about \$1.3 billion to \$1.4 billion worth of that [in the South]." By comparison, between 2002 and 2008, the Army Corps of Engineers spent more than \$4.5 billion on construction projects, most of it base-building, in Afghanistan.

At the site of the future FOB in Shinwar, more than 135 private construction contractors attended what was termed an "Afghan-Coalition contractors rodeo." According to Lieutenant Fernando Roach, a contracting officer with the US Army's Task Force Mountain Warrior, the event was designed "to give potential contractors a walkthrough of the area so they'll have a solid overview of the scope of work." The construction firms then bid on three separate projects: the renovation of the more than thirty-year-old Soviet facilities, the building of new living quarters for Afghan and coalition forces, and the construction of a two-kilometer wall for the base.

In the weeks since the "rodeo," the US Army has announced additional plans to upgrade facilities at other forward operating bases. At FOB Airborne, located near Kane-Ezzat in Wardak Province, for instance, the Army intends to put in reinforced concrete bunkers and blast protection barriers as well as lay concrete foundations for Re-Locatable Buildings (prefabricated, trailer-like structures used for living and working quarters). Similar work is also scheduled for FOB Altimur, an Army camp in Logar Province.

THE AFGHAN BASE BOOM

Recently, the US Army Corps of Engineers, Afghanistan District-Kabul, announced that it would be seeking bids on "site assessments" for Afghan National Security Forces District Headquarters Facilities nationwide. The precise number of Afghan bases scattered throughout the country is unclear.

When asked, Colonel Radmanish of the Afghan Ministry of Defense would state only that major bases were located in Kabul, Pakteya, Kandahar, Herat, and Mazar-e-Sharif, and that ANA units operate all across Afghanistan. Recent US Army contracts for maintenance services provided to Afghan army and police bases, however, suggest that there are no fewer than 300 such facilities that are, according to an ISAF spokesman, not counted among the coalition base inventory.

As opposed to America's fast-food-franchise-filled bases, Afghan ones are often decidedly more rustic affairs. The police headquarters in Khost Farang District, Baghlan Province, is a good example. According to a detailed site assessment conducted by a local contractor for the Army Corps of Engineers and the Afghan government, the district headquarters consists of mud and stone buildings surrounded by a mud wall. The site even lacks a deep well for water. A trench fed by a nearby spring is the only convenient water source.

The US bases that most resemble austere Afghan facilities are combat outposts, also known as COPs. Writing in *Engineering Freedom*, a publication of the Army Corps of Engineers, Environmental Specialist Michael Bell of the Army Corps of Engineers, Afghanistan Engineer District-South's Real Estate Division, recently described the facilities and life on such a base as he and his co-worker, Realty Specialist Damian Salazar, saw it in late 2009:

> COP Sangar ... is a compound surrounded by mud and straw walls. Tents with cots supplied the sleeping quarters ... A medical, pharmacy and command post tent occupied the center of the COP, complete with a few computers with internet access and three primitive operating tables. Showers had just been installed with hot [water] ... only available from 8 a.m. to 10 a.m. and 2 p.m. to 4 p.m ...
>
> An MWR [Morale, Welfare, and Recreation] tent was erected on Thanksgiving Day with an operating television; however, the tent was rarely used due to the cold. Most of the troops used a tent with gym equipment for recreation ... A cook trailer provided a hot simple breakfast and supper. Lunch was MREs [meals ready to eat]. Nights were pitch black with no outside lighting from the base or the city.

WHAT MAKES A BASE?

According to an official site assessment, future construction at the Khost Farang District police headquarters will make use of sand, gravel, and stone, all available on the spot. Additionally, cement, steel, bricks, lime, and gypsum have been located for purchase in Pol-e Khomri City, about eighty-five miles away.

Constructing a base for American troops, however, is another matter. For the far less modest American needs of American troops, builders rely heavily on goods imported over extremely long, difficult to traverse, and sometimes embattled supply lines, all of which adds up to an extraordinarily costly affair. "Our business runs on materials," Lieutenant General Robert Van Antwerp, commander of the Army Corps of Engineers, told an audience at a town hall meeting in Afghanistan in December 2009. "You have to bring in the lumber, you have to bring in the steel, you have to bring in the containers and all that. Transport isn't easy in this country—number one, the roads themselves, number two, coming through other countries to get here—there are just huge challenges in getting the materials here."

To facilitate US base construction projects, a new "virtual storefront"—an online shopping portal—has been launched by the Pentagon's Defense Logistics Agency (DLA). The Maintenance, Repair and Operations Uzbekistan Virtual Storefront website and a defense-contractor-owned-and-operated brick-and-mortar warehouse facility that supports it aim to provide regionally-produced construction materials to speed surge-accelerated building efforts.

From a facility located in Termez, Uzbekistan, cement, concrete, fencing, roofing, rope, sand, steel, gutters, pipe, and other construction materials manufactured in countries like Armenia, Azerbaijan, Georgia, Kazakhstan, Kyrgyzstan, Tajikistan, and Turkmenistan can be rushed to nearby Afghanistan to accelerate base-building efforts. "Having the products closer to the fight will make it easier for warfighters by reducing logistics response and delivery time," says Chet Evanitsky, the DLA's construction and equipment supply chain division chief.

AMERICA'S SHADOWY BASE WORLD

The Pentagon's most recent inventory of bases lists a total of 716 overseas sites. These include facilities owned and leased all across the Middle East as well as a significant presence in Europe and Asia, especially Japan and South Korea. Perhaps even more notable than the Pentagon's impressive public foreign property portfolio are the many sites left off the official inventory. While bases in the Persian Gulf countries of Bahrain, Kuwait, Oman, and the United Arab Emirates are all listed, one conspicuously absent site is

Al-Udeid Air Base, a billion-dollar facility in nearby Qatar, where the US Air Force secretly oversees its ongoing unmanned drone wars.

The count also does not include any sites in Iraq where, as of August 2009, there were still nearly 300 American bases and outposts. Similarly, US bases in Afghanistan—a significant percentage of the 400 foreign sites scattered across the country—are noticeably absent from the Pentagon inventory.

Counting the remaining bases in Iraq—as many as 50 are slated to be operating after President Barack Obama's August 31, 2010 deadline to remove all US "combat troops" from the country—and those in Afghanistan, as well as black sites like Al-Udeid, the total number of US bases overseas now must significantly exceed 1,000. Just exactly how many US military bases (and allied facilities used by US forces) are scattered across the globe may never be publicly known. What we do know—from the experience of bases in Germany, Italy, Japan, and South Korea—is that, once built, they have a tendency toward permanency that a cessation of hostilities, or even outright peace, has a way of not altering.

After nearly a decade of war, close to 700 US, allied, and Afghan military bases dot Afghanistan. Until now, however, they have existed as black sites known to few Americans outside the Pentagon. It remains to be seen, a decade into the future, how many of these sites will still be occupied by US and allied troops and whose flag will be planted on the ever-shifting British-Soviet-US/Afghan site at Shinwar.

16 HOW HEARTS AND MINDS WERE LOST: A PERSONAL EXPERIENCE WORKING WITH THE INTERNATIONAL MILITARY

By Zabih Farhad (pseudonym)

It has been more than eight years since the US-led invasion into Afghanistan that helped bring down the Taliban in late 2001. From my vantage point in Kandahar, the Taliban now seem stronger than ever, having added improvised explosive devices (IEDs) and suicide bombing to their repertoire. There has been much contemplation, in Afghanistan and elsewhere, about what the role of the United States is in Afghanistan. Many Afghans wonder what the US-led invasion has brought them and if the US military is really in Afghanistan to help the Afghan people. US general Stanley McChrystal has declared that the protection of Afghan civilians is more important than the number of Taliban captured. But what does this all mean for ordinary Afghans who have had a mixed experience over the past eight years?

I would like to add to the ongoing debate on the situation in Afghanistan from my own personal experience of working as an interpreter for the US Army for five years, starting at the very impressionable age of seventeen. In the first years after the US invasion of Afghanistan, I tried to show off to my friends during patrols in Kandahar City that I was an interpreter with the US Army—the liberators of Afghanistan. This seems like a long time ago. I would no longer act this way, not only for the sake of my security, but also because I have changed my mind about the role of the US Army in Afghanistan.

I know that there are problems with every organization, and that even bad organizations can have good people in them. I have had a good experience with the US Army, which has impressed me with the discipline among officers (high- and low-ranking alike) and the good behavior toward interpreters. Other armies, such as the British or Dutch, for example, at least from my experience, do not even treat their interpreters well. In an assignment in Helmand, I found out that many British soldiers held all Afghans in contempt, and said things such as, "These [interpreters] are also fucking Afghans."

In an assignment with the Dutch Special Forces, we were not told where we would work until we arrived. Worse, initially we were not allowed to drink water without permission, despite scorching temperatures. After some arguments, we were allowed eight bottles of water a day. My personal belongings, especially notebooks in which I recorded poetry, were searched. After these two experiences, I decided that the only good military were the Americans. But while they treated us interpreters well, their behavior toward the Afghan people was deplorable. This is the reason why ultimately I grew ashamed to work with the US military and decided to leave.

While what I am presenting here is only anecdotal evidence, there are enough of these stories to suggest a serious pattern that may explain why the US military is no longer seen in a good light.

First, there is an issue about whether international military forces provide security to the local population, or endanger their lives. The practice of Forward Operation Bases (FOBs) and other military bases to occupy private land in the vicinity of villages points to the latter. Areas outside the FOBs—often neither clearly marked nor secured—can be used as practice grounds for weapons testing. Sometimes these weapons hit the ground without exploding and are carelessly left behind. Unfortunately, it is often children, sent out in search of wood or water, or to take care of animals, or who are simply curious about these foreigners, who stumble upon these unexploded devices. Many children either have lost body parts or their lives this way. During night-time operations, the use of flares to help light an area has resulted in setting hay and wheat harvests on fire, destroying entire crops. It often takes villages days, if not weeks, to file their complaint and receive a meager compensation.

Second, there is the indirect negative impact on the quality of life of villagers. In an area that already suffered from drought and water shortage, US soldiers, while trying to level a training area, decided to dump dirt inside a hole that belonged to local irrigation systems (*karez*). They would not listen to their Afghan interpreter telling them the *karez* was providing crucial water supplies to surrounding villages. When villagers started to notice that the flow of water to their houses was not only decreasing but also polluted, they went to inspect and found the damage. When they tried to complain to the FOB, villagers were left waiting outside the entry gate for several hours until they were informed they should take their complaint to the governor of the province. This went on for days, weeks, and months— all the while the villages lacked clean drinking water, resulting in many children getting sick.

Third, there is the mistreatment of prisoners. One day, a sergeant of the Afghan National Army (ANA) told me that nobody wanted to guard the detainees at the US Special Forces compound because of a practice to punish those who would not confess with a very terrible kind of "music." The ANA soldiers felt they would lose their minds listening to this music. I had never heard of anything like this—for me, music has only been a pleasant experience. As my experience until then with the US Army had been positive, I thought the ANA sergeant must be joking, so I tried to find a pretext to enter the US Special Forces Base to see for myself. When I came close to where the detainees were held, I indeed heard the music, and even after only a few minutes I could not stand it myself. I was horrified, wondering how people I previously thought very highly of could do something so bad. Some time later, an international friend of mine told me that there was something called "noise torture" or sensory deprivation, which was prohibited under international humanitarian law. I had heard of neither.

After these experiences I decided that I no longer wanted to work with the US Army, or any army for that matter. I once believed that the Americans and other internationals had come to help Afghanistan. Now I am no longer sure. I want to believe the words of General McChrystal that they want to protect the Afghan people, but the track record of the international military so far is so very poor that I am not sure many Afghan villagers who have suffered under past US (or other) military operations are willing to believe there will be a change of strategy. I am not surprised that many villagers have joined the Taliban. I would never do such a thing, but so far I have not had to make the same hard choice that some villagers have. I hope that I will never have to make such a choice, but if forced to, I hope I will be able to go somewhere else.

Part IV THE CASE FOR WITHDRAWAL

17 ALL FOREIGN TROOPS MUST WITHDRAW

An interview with Latif Pedram
by Dominique Bari of *L'Humanité*

Kabul, January 2007. Leader of the non-sectarian opposition, the writer Latif Pedram denounces the military occupation of his country. A former presidential candidate, Pedram leads the National Congress Party (CAN), created in November 2001 to oppose the "Talibanization" of Afghanistan.[1]

L'Humanité: *France has just announced the withdrawal of the 200 members of its Special Forces in Afghanistan, a redeployment of its troops, and a different method of fighting the Taliban. How do you analyze this decision?*

Latif Pedram: It is a way of recognizing that the crisis in Afghanistan has reached a major peak, that the international intervention by the Americans and British is a failure. We can therefore say there is a real internal crisis within the coalition forces. The Europeans, in general, are more and more concerned about the belligerent spiral in which NATO has been caught by multiplying the "clean-up operations" in the south of Afghanistan, with strong support by aerial bombing and its consequent numerous civilian victims. They question the nature of this type of war and its objectives. It is clear that no one believes in the official pretext: the eventual arrest of bin Laden and Mullah Omar.[2] But there is still fear and

---

1   For the program of the National Congress Party, see http://mouv.national.afghan.free.fr/. *Translator's note.*

2   Mullah Omar is the reclusive leader of the Taliban and was Afghanistan's de facto head of state from 1996 to 2001. *Translator's note.*

great anxiety about the prospect of a war that may last years, like in the time of the Soviets. Addressing this reality with clear-headedness may lead gradually to a change of method.

L'Humanité: *Five years after the fall of the Taliban, both President Karzai and the Americans are calling for dialogue with previous Taliban leaders. Do you believe in a future of national reconciliation?*

Latif Pedram: Afghanistan is far from being pacified. Insurgent attacks have reached an unprecedented level of violence, against the background of disillusionment toward a corrupt government. The year 2006 was the most murderous since 2001, with more than 1,000 civilians killed. This return of the Taliban was predictable. When American forces entered Afghan territory, they removed them from power without eliminating them completely; they still needed them to justify their presence and realize their long-term projects, among which was the establishment of permanent military bases. All this allowed the Taliban militias to reorganize rapidly. Today, it is no longer a secret that talks are being pursued with high-level Islamic fundamentalist leaders.

The previous Taliban foreign affairs minister, Wakil Ahmad Mutawakil (notorious for having supported public executions in Kabul stadium), Mullah Dadullah (former defense minister), Mullah Khaksar (one of those formerly responsible for the Taliban information services), Mullah Raketi (often called "Commander Rocket"), and many others are living openly in Kabul. Some of these leaders and other famous murderers during the Taliban regime have seats in the National Assembly.

Under these conditions, Afghans have the right also to wonder what the foreign forces are doing in their country. When preparations are under way for the return of "respectable" Taliban to occupy "respectable" positions of power, is it possible to trust Bush when he asserts that American forces are in the country to build democracy? With whom is he going to build it? Past torturers? At the same time, people have observed what is happening in Iraq, in Palestine, and in Lebanon. Frustration is more and more evident in the general population, and foreign troops are perceived as an occupation force.

L'Humanité: *According to evidence presented by NGOs, daily life has not improved in five years.*

Latif Pedram: After the departure of the Taliban, schools for girls were reopened, but the Karzai regime is part of a restructuring program in line with American liberal logic, and we are in a race to privatize education, healthcare, water, electricity. Public services are deteriorating, public servants trained at the time of the Soviets have been expelled. The cost of living has increased. Basic infrastructure remains deficient. Kabul is full of poor people and beggars, widows seeking hand-outs, very young street vendors and shoe-shiners. Billions of dollars in aid have not been distributed to the right institutions, and corruption is spreading everywhere from drug-trafficking. Opium production has increased by 60 percent this year, and the campaign against opium production is laughable. Everyone knows that numerous politicians and their families, among them the president's younger brother, are directly implicated in this lucrative traffic.

L'Humanité: *How does your Party see a way out of the crisis?*

Latif Pedram: It's not easy; the situation is alarming and the risk of a civil war is real. The solution will have to start with the unconditional withdrawal of foreign military forces, especially American and British, and with the deployment of United Nations forces on the border between Afghanistan and Pakistan. One must reject at all costs the permanent installation of foreign military bases on Afghan soil. Considered as a permanent threat, those bases provide justification for interference in Afghan affairs by all the countries of the region.

L'Humanité: *How to bring an end to the insecurity?*

Latif Pedram: The crisis in Afghanistan also has internal origins, and there won't be any stability if we do not find a solution to the crisis within the country. This is a priority for all the democratic forces, and it means a genuine reconstruction of both State and society in the interests of the most vulnerable Afghans. Poverty also feeds the support for fundamentalism.

It is necessary, moreover, to look closely at the structure of our society, profoundly divided between ethnic groups that have not gone through the same stages of development. For this reason, I am in favor of a federalism established on a regional basis, not on a community basis.

As a non-religious and multi-ethnic movement, our project is based on a national economic cohesion allowing all Afghan ethnic groups to participate in national decision-making. But we have to recognize the realities: the province of Herat and the province of Paktia live a century apart from each other. If the fundamentalists who are powerful in certain provinces of the south oppose the opening of schools in the territory they control, why should they impose their rule in other more advanced provinces? We know that democracy cannot be imposed by force or by bombs; there must be a process of gradual change, and it will take time to create a dynamic of modernization. The conditions have to be right.

18 NO NATION CAN LIBERATE ANOTHER

By Malalai Joya

There is a famous saying: "Injustice anywhere is a threat to justice every-where." Your international solidarity is key. As always, nations are separate from the policymakers. It is the governments that are committing these war crimes. They are betraying democracy, women's rights, and human rights, and they are betraying the truth. The mainstream media is still trying to throw dust in the eyes of democratic people around the world.

You know what your government is doing now? They have put a soft name on the Taliban, these terrorist people, to bring them into power as well. Mullah Omar—this fascist man, this dinosaur—is not in power, and neither is Gulbuddin Hekmatyar, but they want to bring them into power to complete the circle of warlordism and drug-lordism and terrorism in my country.

The US is occupying my country and making a military base there. They are not leaving my country because of their strategy and policies. They don't care about the wishes of my people—how much they are fed up by the situation. Now, my people are sandwiched between two powerful enemies.

Democracy is the alternative for the future of Afghanistan. But there are still many risks for us. Those who tell the truth, those who stand and praise the war against injustice, insecurity, and occupation receive death threats. They get killed or they have to leave Afghanistan. The first casualty is the truth.

Let me say a few things about the role of troops first, since now Obama wants to surge with more troops in Afghanistan. His foreign policy is quite similar to the wrong policy of the Bush administration. It's even worse—according to officials statistics, even more civilians have been killed than during the same time period under Bush.

The worst massacre in Afghanistan from September 11 till now happened during the presidency of Obama. In May 2009, in Farah Province, a bombing killed 150 civilians, most of them women and children. They were even using white phosphorus and cluster bombs. On September 9, 2009, a bombing in Kunduz Province—you may have heard about this through the media—killed 200 civilians, and again, most of them women and children.

Then, after all these crimes, the White House says it apologizes, and Karzai's government—this puppet regime—says thank you. That's it. My people are so fed up that they want an end of the occupation—the end of this so-called war on terror—as soon as possible. As long as these troops are in Afghanistan, the worse the war will be. Through the mainstream media, they are telling you and democratic people around the world that civil war will happen if the US withdraws, but nobody is talking about civil war today.

Nine years ago, the US and its allies invaded Afghanistan under the banner of women's rights. Today, the situation for women—half of the population of the country—is hell in most of the provinces. Killing a woman is as easy as killing a horse. A few days before I came here, in Sar-e Pol Province in the north of Afghanistan, a five-year-old girl was kidnapped and killed. The rape of women and kidnapping and acid attacks—all of this violence is increasing rapidly, even to historical levels. And all of these crimes are happening in the name of democracy, women's rights, and human rights.

I'm saying that as long as these warlords are in power along with these occupation forces, there is no hope to make positive changes in the lives of the men and women of my country.

It's not only women who are suffering. If I talked only about conditions for women, it would take all morning, but I wouldn't even be finished. All of this shocking news that the media never gives to the people around the world. Women don't even have a human life.

But today, women *and* men don't have liberation. Millions of Afghans suffer from injustice, insecurity, corruption, joblessness, etc. Your government says that it sent troops there so that girls can go to school, but according to official figures from the government, more than 600 schools have been closed. When the girls go to school, they throw acid in their faces.

I think education is important—very important in my country. I always say that it's the key to our emancipation. But security is more important than food and water. They keep the situation dangerous like this so they can stay longer in Afghanistan, because of their strategy and policies.

To know more about the deep tragedy of Afghanistan: during these nine years, they changed my country to the capital of the center of the drug trade. Today, 93 percent of opium produced in the world is from Afghanistan. The brother of Hamid Karzai, Ahmed Wali Karzai, is a famous drug trafficker, as the *New York Times* recently wrote. Through the dirty business of opium, every year, $500 million goes into the pocket of the Taliban alone. And since 2001, there has been a 4,500 percent increase in opium. If the US government doesn't stop this wrong policy, the drugs will find their way onto the streets of New York, and destroy the lives of youth here as well.

Another example of the catastrophic situation of my country is that in 2009, the United Nations human development index ranked Afghanistan 181st out of 182 countries. This is a country where the government received $36 billion over the past years, according to official reports. Where did that money go? Into pockets of warlords and drug lords—these criminals and misogynists.

Today, eighteen million people of my country live on less than $2 a day. Mothers in Herat and Ghor provinces are ready to sell their babies for $10 because they cannot feed them. And this is another example of many shocking examples that never made it into the mainstream media.

My people are caught now between two powerful enemies, and they are being crushed. From the sky, the bombs of the occupation forces are falling, killing civilians. And on the ground, there is the Taliban, and also these warlords. So we have three kinds of enemies. But the withdrawal of one enemy—these US occupation forces whose government sends them to war, and also supports the corrupt mafia system of Hamid Karzai with more money and men—will make it much easier to fight the enemies that are left.

I promise I will never be tired as long as war is in Afghanistan as well as in other countries—what is going on in Iraq, in Burma, in Pakistan, in Palestine. The list can be longer. No nation can bring liberation to another nation. These are nations that can liberate themselves. The nations that pose themselves as liberators to others will lead them into slavery. What we have experienced in Afghanistan and in Iraq prove this point.

If the US and its allies let us have a little bit of space and peace, then we know what to do with our destiny. The people of Afghanistan don't want occupation. They need honest support, they need educational support, they need your powerful voice—which means, first of all, international solidarity against the warmongers of your government.

Regarding Barack Obama and the Nobel Peace Prize, they are giving the Peace Prize to the president of war—who is waging war in Afghanistan, in Iraq, and in Pakistan, and is also supporting the criminal regime of Israel and what is going on today in Palestine. Many heroes and heroines are risking their lives and doing a lot for peace, but nobody knows their name. They must be nominated for the prize. I think the question for Obama is, after nine months, what did he do for peace that he received this Nobel Peace Prize?

And in such a disastrous situation, they are talking about so-called democratic elections. I think you would agree with us that an election under the shadow of guns, warlordism, drug-lordism, awful corruption, and occupation forces has no legitimacy at all. There's a famous saying that it's not important who's voting, it's important who is counting. That's our problem. Some democrats ran for the election in Afghanistan, but all the ballot boxes are in the hands of mafia. They betrayed the vote of my people.

Before the results of the election, people in my country said to each other that the result will be like the same donkey—I don't mean to be insulting to donkeys—but with a new saddle. Everyone knows that the winner of the election will be picked by the White House.

There's a huge difference between the presidential election and the parliamentary and provincial elections. For the parliamentary election, we have some chance for democrats to run, and that is my message to my people. If a few of us are allowed, it's good to be in these national bodies to be a small voice of our people. As I experienced, in this parliament, I said it was worse than animals—that it's like a zoo. These criminals told me that I must apologize for this comment. I said that I must apologize to the animals that I insult.

Don't misunderstand—in our parliament, we have a few democrats, men and women. Unfortunately you can count them very quickly, but it's good to be the voice of the people. But for the presidential election, we have one choice—the person who will be the next puppet.

Do not be deceived with this melodrama of a so-called democratic election—I think it's the most ridiculous election anywhere in the world. They spent $250 million on the election, while people do not have enough food to eat. Less than 10 percent of people participated in the election. And now they want to waste more money. That's why we believe that your government and NATO are wasting taxpayer money and the blood of your soldiers in Afghanistan by supporting such a terrorist.

I gave only a few examples of the disastrous situation of my country. I'm saying that my people can liberate themselves. But we need your helping hand. As always, I again stress that we separate people from the policy-makers of their government. We are honored that we have the support of democratic-minded, peace-loving people in the US. But we need more of your solidarity and support for our country.

Let me conclude my speech with a quote from Bertolt Brecht, who said that "Those who struggle may fail, but those who do not struggle have already failed." Thanks a lot for your solidarity and support.

19 WHAT OBAMA COULD LEARN FROM GORBACHEV

By Robert Crews

Is Afghanistan the new Vietnam? From the White House to the Pentagon and the Beltway glitterati, historical analogies are all the rage. Legions of strategists are beefing up their Iraqi-inspired schemes with lessons from the Vietnamese jungles.

These renewed debates about Vietnam are so striking because they reflect an unwillingness to engage with the politics and history of the country where American and NATO troops are actually fighting and dying. No period of Afghan history is more relevant than that defined by the war with the Soviet Union. Yet most Americans still view it through the Hollywood lens: *Rambo III* and *Charlie Wilson's War* made Americans the central heroes who successfully deployed their Afghan pawns to bring down the "Evil Empire."

What could we learn from revisiting the Soviet experience through more sober eyes? Historical comparisons offer no magical solutions to complex political problems, but in this case they suggest ways to arrive at a deeper understanding of the forces that have transformed Afghan society over the past thirty years.

First, the story of the Soviet–Afghan War challenges the view that Afghanistan is a timeless "graveyard of empires." The war itself was a catalyst for dramatic change. Soviet arms robbed the country of more than a million people and scattered millions more—including most of its educated elites. They decimated its infrastructure and critical sectors of the state and economy. Soviet policies empowered minority communities. Tribal and ethnic identities rapidly shifted in response. For their part, the mujahideen, armed and backed by the US even before the Soviet invasion, left a deep mark on the Afghan social fabric, not least by eliminating secular opposition figures. Poppies, landmines, and cheap guns were the fruits of Cold War "victory." The Taliban movement was another. The country has not recovered.

Second, though it is commonplace to be scornful of the Soviet venture in Afghanistan, it is critical to recognize the structural dynamic that now makes the position of the US closely resemble that of the Soviets in the 1980s. The USSR was a one-party dictatorship, and its forces showed far less restraint toward civilian populations than US and NATO troops. In Afghanistan, however, the differences narrow.

Moscow and Washington became embroiled there because their elites calculated that great power interests were at stake on the Hindu Kush. Both claimed self-defense (against al Qaeda terrorism and US "imperialism," respectively), even as they failed to grasp the nature of the foe: in one case a small but spatially diffuse, global network of militants loosely joined together by anti-imperialist ideals; in the other a superpower with little capacity, as it turns out, to govern the region.

More important, the challenges confronted by the superpowers resemble one another in that both became trapped—not by supposedly primordial tribes, Afghanistan's jagged terrain, or even by the "rage" of jihad—but by their own Afghan proxies who spoke the languages of socialism and democracy, but who pursued their independent interests. The Soviets intervened in December 1979 to back Afghan communists who had seized power in April 1978, and who ruthlessly set upon their enemies and violently unleashed a revolution to end feudalism and liberate women. But the KGB repeatedly expressed exasperation at their inability to control the Afghan communists or temper their radicalism. The Afghan communists' brutal detentions, torture, and murder compounded the Soviets' troubles by stoking the resistance.

In Hamid Karzai, the US has created a similar liability. American troops find themselves fighting for a government whom many, if not most, Afghans regard as illegitimate. The fault lies not with the Afghans alone, but with the great powers who, forgetting the history of colonialism, mistakenly believed they could govern through intermediaries who lack support within their own societies.

Lastly, the Soviet defeat should evoke cautious humility rather than schadenfreude. The Soviets enjoyed the logistical advantage of fighting in a neighboring country. They had personnel, including Uzbeks and Tajiks, who knew Afghan languages and who had local ties and experience. The US faces a logistical and intelligence nightmare, and is struggling to identify an enemy that is formidable even without a superpower patron.

The Soviet–Afghan War also bears practical lessons for the current US escalation. In detaining Afghans in the lawless environs of Bagram, conducting aerial raids (including drone attacks), and pledging more than a billion dollars for uncontrollable "tribal militias," the US is repeating the worst Soviet mistakes. Backed by a vast complex of social scientists, journalists, and think-tank pundits, American elites hold fast to the view that the military can remake foreign countries at will. Whether fighting Vietnamese, Iraqis, Afghans, or Pakistanis, they imagine that heterogeneous political scenarios can be subsumed under the single, universal rubric of "counterinsurgency," with a military solution always close at hand.

Some Soviet authorities knew better. The US would do well to listen to them now. One is a September 1979 KGB memo calling for pressure on the Afghan leadership to create a broad-based coalition government, including the opposition. Another is Gorbachev's plan of 1986 to extricate the USSR by pursuing national reconciliation and international diplomacy. The US has tragically neglected these approaches, narrowly seeking a military victory and ignoring Afghanistan's complicated past.

20 OBAMA'S POLICIES MAKE THE SITUATION WORSE

By Graham Fuller

For all the talk of "smart power," President Obama is pressing down the same path of failure in Pakistan marked out by George Bush. The realities suggest a need for drastic revision of US strategic thinking.

- Military force will not win the day in either Afghanistan or Pakistan; crises have only grown worse under the US military footprint.

- The Taliban represent zealous and largely ignorant mountain Islamists. They are also all ethnic Pashtuns. Most Pashtuns see the Taliban—like them or not—as the primary vehicle for restoration of Pashtun power in Afghanistan, lost in 2001. Pashtuns are also among the most fiercely nationalist, tribalized, and xenophobic peoples of the world, united only against the foreign invader. In the end, the Taliban are probably more Pashtun than they are Islamist.

- It is a fantasy to think of ever sealing the Pakistan–Afghanistan border. The "Durand Line" is an arbitrary imperial line drawn through Pashtun tribes on both sides of the border. And there are twice as many Pashtuns in Pakistan as there are in Afghanistan. The struggle of thirteen million Afghan Pashtuns has already inflamed Pakistan's twenty-eight million Pashtuns.

- India is the primary geopolitical threat to Pakistan, not Afghanistan. Pakistan must therefore always maintain Afghanistan as a friendly state. India furthermore is intent upon gaining a serious foothold in Afghanistan—in the intelligence, economic, and political arenas—that chills Islamabad.

– Pakistan will therefore never rupture ties or abandon the Pashtuns, in either country, whether radical Islamist or not. Pakistan can never afford to have Pashtuns hostile to Islamabad in control of Kabul, or at home.

– Occupation everywhere creates hatred, as the US is learning. Yet Pashtuns remarkably have not been part of the jihadi movement at the international level, although many are indeed quick to ally themselves at home with al Qaeda against the US military.

– The US had every reason to strike back at the al Qaeda presence in Afghanistan after the outrage of 9/11. The Taliban were furthermore poster children for an incompetent and harsh regime. But the Taliban retreated from, rather than lost, the war in 2001, in order to fight another day. Indeed, one can debate whether it might have been possible—with sustained pressure from Pakistan, Iran, Saudi Arabia, and almost all other Muslim countries that viewed the Taliban as primitives—to force the Taliban to yield up al Qaeda over time without war. That debate is in any case now moot. But the consequences of that war are baleful, debilitating, and *still* spreading.

– The situation in Pakistan has gone from bad to worse as a direct consequence of the US war raging on the Afghan border. US policy has now carried the Afghan War over the border into Pakistan with its incursions, drone bombings, and assassinations—the classic response to a failure to deal with insurgency in one country. Remember the invasion of Cambodia to save Vietnam?

– The deeply entrenched Islamic and tribal character of Pashtun rule in the North-West Frontier Province in Pakistan will not be transformed by invasion or war. The task requires probably several generations to start to change the deeply embedded social and psychological character of the area. War induces visceral and atavistic responses.

– Pakistan is indeed now beginning to crack under the relentless pressure directly exerted by the US. Anti-American impulses in Pakistan are at high pitch, strengthening Islamic radicalism and forcing reluctant acquiescence to it even by non-Islamists.

Only the withdrawal of American and NATO boots on the ground will begin to allow the process of near-frantic emotions to subside within Pakistan, and for the region to start to cool down. Pakistan is experienced in governance and is well able to deal with its own Islamists and tribalists under normal circumstances; until recently, Pakistani Islamists had one of the lowest rates of electoral success in the Muslim world.

But US policies have now driven local nationalism, xenophobia, and Islamism to combined fever pitch. As Washington demands that Pakistan redeem failed American policies in Afghanistan, Islamabad can no longer manage its domestic crisis.

The Pakistani army is more than capable of maintaining state power against tribal militias and to defend its own nukes. Only a convulsive nationalist revolutionary spirit could change that—something most Pakistanis do not want. But Washington can still succeed in destabilizing Pakistan if it perpetuates its present hard-line strategies. A new chapter of military rule—not what Pakistan needs—will be the likely result, and even then Islamabad's basic policies will not change, except at the cosmetic level.

In the end, only moderate Islamists themselves can prevail over the radicals whose main source of legitimacy comes from inciting popular resistance against the external invader. Sadly, US forces and Islamist radicals are now approaching a state of co-dependency.

It would be heartening to see a solid working democracy established in Afghanistan. Or widespread female rights and education—areas where Soviet occupation ironically did rather well. But these changes are not going to happen even within one generation, given the history of social and economic devastation of the country over thirty years.

Al Qaeda's threat no longer emanates from the caves of the borderlands, but from its symbolism that has long since metastasized to other activists of the Muslim world. Meanwhile, the Pashtuns will fight on for a major national voice in Afghanistan. But few Pashtuns on either side of the border will long maintain a radical and international jihadi perspective once the incitement of the US presence is gone. Nobody on either side of the border really wants it.

What can be done must be consonant with the political culture. Let non-military and neutral international organizations, free of geopolitical taint, take over the binding of Afghan wounds and the building of state structures.

If the past nine years had shown ongoing success, perhaps an alternative case for US policies could be made. But the evidence on the ground demonstrates only continued deterioration and darkening of the prognosis. Will we have more of the same? Or will there be a US recognition that the American presence has now become more the problem than the solution? We do not hear that debate.

21 THE WAR WE CAN'T WIN: THE LIMITS OF AMERICAN POWER

By Andrew J. Bacevich

History deals rudely with the pretensions of those who presume to determine its course. In an American context, this describes the fate of those falling prey to the Wilsonian Conceit. Yet the damage done by that conceit outlives its perpetrators.

From time to time, in some moment of peril or anxiety, a statesman appears on the scene promising to eliminate tyranny, ensure the triumph of liberty, and achieve permanent peace. For a moment, the statesman achieves the status of prophet, one who in his own person seemingly embodies the essence of the American purpose. Then reality intrudes, exposing the promises as costly fantasies. The prophet's followers abandon him. Mocked and reviled, he is eventually banished—perhaps to some gated community in Dallas.

Yet however brief his ascendancy, the discredited prophet leaves behind a legacy. Most obvious are the problems created and left unresolved, commitments made and left unfulfilled, debts accrued and left unpaid. Less obvious, but for that reason more important, are the changes in perception.

The prophet recasts our image of reality. Long after his departure, remnants of that image linger and retain their capacity to beguile: consider how the Wilsonian vision of the United States as crusader state called upon to redeem the world in World War I has periodically resurfaced despite Woodrow Wilson's own manifest failure to make good on that expectation. The prophet declaims and departs. Yet traces of his testimony, however at odds with the facts, remain lodged in our consciousness.

166 ANDREW J. BACEVICH

So it is today with Afghanistan, the conflict that George W. Bush began, then ignored, and finally bequeathed to his successor. Barack Obama has embraced that conflict as "the war we must win." Those who celebrated Bush's militancy back in the intoxicating days when he was promising to rid the world of evil see Obama's enthusiasm for pressing on in Afghanistan as a vindication of sorts. They are right to do so.

The misguided and mismanaged global war on terror reduced Bush's presidency to ruin. The candidate whose run for high office derived its energy from an implicit promise to repudiate all that Bush had wrought now seems intent on salvaging something useful from that failed enterprise— even if that means putting his own presidency at risk. When it comes to Afghanistan, Obama may be singing in a different key, but to anyone with an ear for music—especially for military marches—the melody remains intact.

Candidate Obama once derided the notion that the United States is called upon to determine the fate of Iraq. President Obama expresses a willingness to expend untold billions—not to mention who knows how many lives—in order to determine the fate of Afghanistan. Liberals may have interpreted Obama's campaign pledge to ramp up the US military commitment to Afghanistan as calculated to insulate himself from the charge of being a national-security wimp. Events have exposed that interpretation as incorrect. It turns out—apparently—that the president genuinely views this remote, landlocked, primitive Central Asian country as a vital US national-security interest.

What is it about Afghanistan, possessing next to nothing that the United States requires, that justifies such lavish attention? In Washington, this question goes not only unanswered but unasked. Among Democrats and Republicans alike, with few exceptions, Afghanistan's importance is simply assumed—much the way fifty years ago otherwise intelligent people simply assumed that the United States had a vital interest in ensuring the survival of South Vietnam. As then, so today, the assumption does not stand up to even casual scrutiny.

Tune in to the Sunday talk shows or consult the op-ed pages and you might conclude otherwise. Those who profess to be in the know insist that the fight in Afghanistan is essential to keeping America safe. The events of September 11, 2001, ostensibly occurred because we ignored Afghanistan.

Preventing the recurrence of those events, therefore, requires that we fix the place.

Yet this widely accepted line of reasoning overlooks the primary reason why the 9/11 conspiracy succeeded: federal, state, and local agencies responsible for basic security fell down on the job, failing to install even minimally adequate security measures in the nation's airports. The national-security apparatus wasn't paying attention—indeed, it ignored or downplayed all sorts of warning signs, not least of all Osama bin Laden's declaration of war against the United States. Consumed with its ABC agenda—"anything but Clinton" was the Bush administration's watchword in those days—the people at the top didn't have their eye on the ball. So we let ourselves get sucker-punched. Averting a recurrence of that awful day does not require the semi-permanent occupation and pacification of distant countries like Afghanistan. Rather, it requires that the United States erect and maintain robust defenses.

Fixing Afghanistan is not only unnecessary, it's also likely to prove impossible. Not for nothing has the place acquired the nickname the "graveyard of empires". Of course, Americans, insistent that the dominion over which they preside does not meet the definition of empire, evince little interest in how Brits, Russians, or other foreigners have fared in attempting to impose their will on the Afghans. As General David McKiernan, until just recently the US commander in Afghanistan, put it, "There's always an inclination to relate what we're doing with previous nations," adding, "I think that's a very unhealthy comparison." McKiernan was expressing a view common among the ranks of the political and military elite: We're Americans. We're different. Therefore, the experience of others does not apply.

Of course, Americans like McKiernan who reject as irrelevant the experience of others might at least be willing to contemplate the experience of the United States itself. Take the case of Iraq, now bizarrely trumpeted in some quarters as a "success" and even more bizarrely seen as offering a template for how to turn Afghanistan around.

Much has been made of the United States Army's rediscovery of (and growing infatuation with) counterinsurgency doctrine, applied in Iraq beginning in late 2006 when President Bush announced his so-called surge and anointed General David Petraeus as the senior US commander in Baghdad. Yet technique is no substitute for strategy. Violence in Iraq may be down, but evidence of the promised political reconciliation that the surge was intended to produce remains elusive. America's Mesopotamian misadventure continues.

Pretending that the surge has redeemed the Iraq war is akin to claiming that when Andy Jackson "caught the bloody British in the town of New Orleans" he thereby enabled the United States to emerge victorious from the War of 1812. Such a judgment works well as folklore but ignores an abundance of contrary evidence.

Six-plus years after it began, Operation Iraqi Freedom has consumed something like a trillion dollars—with the meter still running—and has taken the lives of more than forty-three hundred American soldiers. Meanwhile, in Baghdad and other major Iraqi cities, car bombs continue to detonate at regular intervals, killing and maiming dozens. Anyone inclined to put Iraq in the nation's rearview mirror is simply deluded. Not long ago General Raymond Odierno, Petraeus's successor and the fifth US commander in Baghdad, expressed the view that the insurgency in Iraq is likely to drag on for another five, ten, or fifteen years. Events may well show that Odierno is an optimist.

Given the embarrassing yet indisputable fact that this was an utterly needless war—no Iraqi weapons of mass destruction found, no ties between Saddam Hussein and the jihadists established, no democratic transformation of the Islamic world set in motion, no road to peace in Jerusalem discovered in downtown Baghdad—to describe Iraq as a success, and as a model for application elsewhere, is nothing short of obscene. The great unacknowledged lesson of Iraq is the one that the writer Norman Mailer identified decades ago: "Fighting a war to fix something works about as good as going to a whorehouse to get rid of a clap."

For those who, despite all this, still hanker to have a go at nation-building, why start with Afghanistan? Why not first fix, say, Mexico? In terms of its importance to the United States, our southern neighbor—a major supplier of oil and drugs, among other commodities deemed vital to the American way of life—outranks Afghanistan by several orders of magnitude.

If one believes that moral considerations rather than self-interest should inform foreign policy, Mexico still qualifies for priority attention. Consider the theft of California. Or consider more recently how the American appetite for illicit drugs and our liberal gun laws have corroded Mexican institutions and produced an epidemic of violence afflicting ordinary Mexicans. We owe these people, big time.

Yet any politician calling for the commitment of 60,000 US troops to Mexico to secure those interests or acquit those moral obligations would be laughed out of Washington—and rightly so. Any pundit proposing that the United States assume responsibility for eliminating the corruption that is endemic in Mexican politics while establishing in Mexico City effective mechanisms of governance would have his license to pontificate revoked. Anyone suggesting that the United States possesses the wisdom and the wherewithal to solve the problem of Mexican drug trafficking, to endow Mexico with competent security forces, and to reform the Mexican school system (while protecting the rights of Mexican women), would be dismissed as a lunatic. Meanwhile, those who promote such programs for Afghanistan, ignoring questions of cost and ignoring as well the corruption and ineffectiveness that pervade our own institutions, are treated like sages.

The contrast between Washington's preoccupation with Afghanistan and its relative indifference to Mexico testifies to the distortion of US national security priorities induced by George W. Bush in his post-9/11 prophetic mode—distortions now being endorsed by Bush's successor. It also testifies to a vast failure of imagination to which our governing classes have succumbed.

This failure of imagination makes it literally impossible for those who possess either authority or influence in Washington to consider the possibility (a) that the solution to America's problems is to be found not out there—where "there" in this case is Central Asia—but here at home; (b) that the people out there, rather than requiring our ministrations, may well be capable of managing their own affairs relying on their own methods; and (c) that to disregard (a) and (b) is to open the door to great mischief and in all likelihood to perpetrate no small amount of evil.

Needless to say, when mischief or evil does occur—when a stray American bomb kills a few dozen Afghan civilians, for instance—the costs of this failure of imagination are not borne by the people who inhabit the leafy neighborhoods of northwest Washington, who lunch at the Palm or the Metropolitan Club and school their kids at Sidwell Friends. So the answer to the question of the hour—what should the United States do about Afghanistan?—comes down to this: a sense of realism and a sense of proportion should oblige us to take a minimalist approach. As with Uruguay or Fiji or Estonia or other countries where US interests are limited, the United States should undertake to secure those interests at the lowest cost possible.

What might this mean in practice? General Petraeus, now commanding United States Central Command, commented in a May 2009 interview that "the mission is to ensure that Afghanistan does not again become a sanctuary for al Qaeda and other transnational extremists," in effect "to deny them safe havens in which they can plan and train for such attacks."

The mission statement is a sound one. The current approach to accomplishing the mission is not sound and, indeed, qualifies as counterproductive. Note that denying al Qaeda safe havens in Pakistan hasn't required US forces to occupy the frontier regions of that country. Similarly, denying al Qaeda safe havens in Afghanistan shouldn't require military occupation by the United States and its allies.

It would be much better to let local authorities do the heavy lifting. Provided with appropriate incentives, the tribal chiefs who actually run Afghanistan are best positioned to prevent terrorist networks from establishing a large-scale presence. As a backup, intensive surveillance complemented with precision punitive strikes (assuming we can manage to kill the right people) will suffice to disrupt al Qaeda's plans. Certainly, that approach offers a cheaper and more efficient alternative to establishing a large-scale and long-term US ground presence—which, as the US campaigns in both Iraq and Afghanistan have demonstrated, has the unintended effect of handing jihadists a recruiting tool that they are quick to exploit.

In the immediate wake of 9/11, all the talk—much of it emanating from neoconservative quarters—was about achieving a "decisive victory" over terror. The reality is that we can't eliminate every last armed militant harboring a grudge against the West. Nor do we need to. As long as we maintain adequate defenses, al Qaeda operatives, hunkered down in their caves, pose no more than a modest threat. As for the Taliban, unless they manage to establish enclaves in places like New Jersey or Miami, the danger they pose to the United States falls several notches below the threat posed by Cuba, which is no threat at all.

As for the putatively existential challenge posed by Islamic radicalism, that project will prove ultimately to be a self-defeating one. What violent Islamists have on offer—a rejection of modernity that aims to restore the caliphate and unify the *ummah* [community]—doesn't sell. In this regard, Iran—its nuclear aspirations the subject of much hand-wringing—offers considerable cause for hope. Much like the Castro revolution that once elicited so much angst in Washington, the Islamic revolution launched in 1979 has failed resoundingly. Observers once feared that the revolution inspired and led by the Ayatollah Khomeini would sweep across the Persian Gulf. In fact, it has accomplished precious little. Within Iran itself, the Islamic republic no longer represents the hopes and aspirations of the Iranian people, as the tens of thousands of protesters who recently filled the streets of Tehran and other Iranian cities made evident. Here we see foretold the fate awaiting the revolutionary cause that Osama bin Laden purports to promote.

In short, time is on our side, not on the side of those who proclaim their intention of turning back the clock to the fifteenth century. The ethos of consumption and individual autonomy, privileging the here and now over the eternal, will conquer the Muslim world as surely as it is conquering East Asia and as surely as it has already conquered what was once known as Christendom.

It's the wreckage left in the wake of that conquest that demands our attention. If the United States today has a saving mission, it is to save itself. Speaking in the midst of another unnecessary war back in 1967, Martin Luther King got it exactly right: "Come home, America." The prophet of that era urged his countrymen to take on "the triple evils of racism, economic exploitation, and militarism."

Dr. King's list of evils may need a bit of tweaking—in our own day, the sins requiring expiation number more than three. Yet in his insistence that we first heal ourselves, King remains today the prophet we ignore at our peril. That Barack Obama should fail to realize this qualifies as not only ironic but inexplicable.

22 HOW TO GET OUT

By Robert Dreyfuss

There is no likelihood that the current US war in Afghanistan can achieve its aims (a narrower goal, the elimination of al Qaeda, has for the most part already been accomplished). The corrupt government of President Karzai and his cronies is no longer sustainable, whether or not there is a second round in the fraud-marred election. A new government in Kabul must emerge, in the process accommodating Pashtun nationalists, the Taliban, and other insurgents. Those latter groups, along with tribal and ethnic leaders, various warlords, and representatives of Afghanistan's myriad political factions, will need international support to underwrite a new national compact. That national accord will probably not be a strong central government but rather a decentralized federal system, in which provinces and districts retain a significant degree of autonomy. To secure international support, the United States must defer to the United Nations to convene a conference in which Afghans themselves hammer out the new way forward. The world community must pledge its support of Afghanistan financially for years to come. And this must occur against the backdrop of an unconditional withdrawal of US and NATO forces.

Accordingly, the first step for Washington must be to abandon the idea of a decades-long counterinsurgency, fire its advocates—including General Stanley McChrystal and General David Petraeus, architect of the *Counterinsurgency Field Manual*—and admit that the multi-headed insurgency in southern and eastern Afghanistan can't be defeated by military means. At the same time the Obama administration will have to give up its massive nation-building project, dismantling the empire of US departments, agencies, provincial reconstruction teams, and the rest, now overseen by Richard Holbrooke, the US special envoy. Instead, the United States should prepare to channel a substantial flow of international development assistance and humanitarian aid to Afghanistan through a newly reconstructed, rebalanced Afghan government.

In addition, President Obama should declare that the United States has achieved its principal objective in Afghanistan, namely, the near-total destruction of al Qaeda as an organization. With the agreement of the Afghan government, a limited US intelligence and counterterrorism mission designed to monitor the remnants of al Qaeda can remain in Afghanistan. And al Qaeda's operations in Afghanistan and Pakistan can be dealt with by intelligence, law enforcement, and US Special Forces personnel in cooperation with security agencies in those countries.

The president must also announce an unconditional timetable for the withdrawal of US and NATO forces, on the model of the US drawdown in Iraq, over, say, a period of two years or so. The goal should be a Status of Forces Agreement with a new Afghan government, pertaining to the role of US forces in training an Afghan national army far smaller than the bulky 400,000-man security force envisioned by General McChrystal.

Then comes the tricky part: the president should encourage the convening of an international Bonn II conference involving the UN, the major world powers, and Afghanistan's neighbors—including Iran, India, and Pakistan—to support the renegotiation of the Afghanistan compact. At the table must be representatives of all of Afghanistan's stakeholders, including the Taliban and their allies. In advance of that, the United States should join other nations and the UN to persuade President Karzai, his main electoral opponents, and other Afghan politicians to form a coalition that would create an interim caretaker regime until the establishment of a more broadly based government.

At the same time, the United States must launch a diplomatic surge aimed at persuading, cajoling, and bribing Afghanistan's neighbors to support the effort, including Taliban supporters, such as Pakistan and Saudi Arabia, and opponents, including Iran, India, and Russia. Obama must recognize that Pakistan is a key part of the problem, not the solution: the Afghan Taliban are not a formless, leaderless group. They are a branch of Pakistan's army and its intelligence service, the ISI, and they have an address: Rawalpindi, the garrison city that is the headquarters for the Pakistani military. The message of the world community to the Pakistani military must be clear: Pakistan's legitimate interests in Afghanistan will be recognized, but Pakistani support of terrorist groups, whether aimed at Afghanistan or Kashmir, is simply not acceptable.

As a central part of the diplomatic effort, Obama must strongly encourage Pakistan and Saudi Arabia to bring key elements of the three interlinked insurgency movements—the Taliban, the Hezb-i-Islami of Gulbuddin Hekmatyar, and the Haqqani network—to the bargaining table. Elements of those groups that opt not to participate are unlikely to present more than a nuisance challenge to the government in Kabul, if cut off from Pakistani support. China, Pakistan's ally, which has a vital interest in Central Asia, should be willing to use its influence in Pakistan to make sure Islamabad and Rawalpindi are on board.

Similarly, Obama will have to work to get Iran, India, and Russia to help persuade the remnants of the anti-Taliban Northern Alliance (mostly Tajiks, Uzbeks, and Hazaras) to make room in Kabul for an enlarged Pashtun role, including the Taliban, in what could become a stable power-sharing arrangement. The ongoing US–Iran talks can be a useful forum to reach agreement between Washington and Tehran on common interests in stabilizing Afghanistan.

Last, the United States must take the lead in creating a global Marshall Plan to help Afghanistan rebuild its war-shattered economy, build a passable infrastructure, and establish the rudiments of a national government. The United States must be realistic about what it can accomplish—and what it cannot. It cannot remake Afghan society, change its cultural mores, modernize its religious outlook, educate its women, or reshape the tribal system that prevails in its rural villages. It can break al Qaeda and, as it exits, leave behind at least the possibility that Afghans will begin to create a sustainable society. But it must recognize, above all, that what it leaves behind won't be pretty.

A NOTE ON SOURCES

Most of the articles in this book are either reportage or opinion pieces. In both cases, they not surprisingly lack footnotes. The works first published at TomDispatch.com generally contain today's democratized footnote—the hyperlink, which instantly transports the reader to the source material or more in-depth readings on the topic. However, long strings of URLs are functionally useless when removed from the web and so are not reproduced in this book. Instead, readers interested in what the citations in these pieces have to offer are encouraged to seek out the originals online.

ACKNOWLEDGMENTS

Writing the acknowledgments for a collection of articles by more than twenty authors is a little like being a producer at a movie award ceremony who takes the bows for the more important work of a talented cast and crew, without letting any of them get a word in edgewise. Still, the task falls to me, so, on behalf of all the authors, I would like to thank the people who guided and inspired their work, ultimately making this book possible.

Next, I want to offer my own thanks to all the authors who contributed to this collection. I appreciate the graciousness of each of them in allowing me to reprint his or her work. I thank them all for their insights and analysis, which helped me grapple with the crucial issues this collection confronts.

It's no accident that a significant number of contributors to this volume write for the Nation Institute's TomDispatch.com. As an associate editor of the site, I have had the pleasure of reading and editing so many of their excellent works—on Afghanistan and other topics—over the years. Not surprisingly, a number of important works published at the site sprang to mind as soon as I began to assemble this collection of voices. I only regret the limitations of space, since there were many others I would have liked to include.

"Tom" of TomDispatch.com is friend and editor-extraordinaire Tom Engelhardt. There are few things that I write that don't bear some imprint of Tom's judicious editorial skills, insights, or advice. He was instrumental in paving the way for many author permissions, and offered so much instrumental input that his name should probably appear on the cover. What can I say but: "Talk to you tomorrow, if not later today"?

I owe special thanks to Ann Jones and Robert Crews, who pointed me toward articles I otherwise would have missed, and to Chalmers Johnson and Sara Bershtel at Metropolitan Books, who granted permission to use an article that will also appear in Chalmers' latest book, *Dismantling the Empire.*

A special debt of gratitude goes to Wendy Kristiansen at the English-language edition of *Le Monde diplomatique*, Isabella de Vega at Agence Global, Adam Mendelson at *The Middle East Journal*, Lara McCoy at Rbth.ru, Hervé Fuyet at *L'Humanité in English*, and Habiba Alcindor at *The Nation*. I owe many thanks, as well, to Tony Wood, the Deputy Editor of *New Left Review* who searched high and low for just the right article to offer a glimpse of the Soviet occupation of Afghanistan. He and Tariq Ali also provided helpful insights that shaped this collection.

I would have never had the opportunity to edit this book without Jacob Stevens at Verso. Jake's confidence in my work, as well as his patience, advice, and keen eye have been invaluable. He helped make this a broader, more comprehensive collection, and for that I am extremely grateful.

I owe my parents a debt of gratitude and especially want to say, "Thanks, Dad," for recommending two articles I had already slated for the book. Great minds and all that . . .

Finally, where would I be without Tam? Thanks for seeing me through this and so many other projects, for acting as a sounding board, an editor and my *consigliere*. You are everything to me and make my life worthwhile.

Grateful acknowledgment is made to the following for allowing permission to reprint previously published material:

© 2008 *New Left Review*. Map of Afghanistan. First published by *New Left Review*, March–April 2008.

© 2009 Juan Cole. "Armageddon at the Top of the World: A Century of Frenzy over the North-West Frontier" by Juan Cole. First published at TomDispatch.com, July 27, 2009.

© 2009 Rodric Braithwaite. "The Familiar Road to Failure in Afghanistan" by Rodric Braithwaite. First published by *Financial Times*, December 21, 2009.

© 2010 Elena Bonner. Excerpts from *Memoirs* by Andrei Sakharov. Translated by Richard Lourie (London: Hutchinson/Knopf, 1990).

© 2010 Nezavisimoe Voennoe Obozrenie. "We Were Waging War Against a People" by Oleg Vasilevich Kustov. First printed in *Nezavisimoe Voennoe Obozrenie*, January 29, 2010. Translated by Tony Wood.

© 2010 Chalmers Johnson. "Blowback World" from *Dismantling The Empire* by Chalmers Johnson. Reprinted by arrangement with Henry Holt and Company, LLC. A slightly different version of this article first appeared as "Abolish the CIA!" in the *London Review of Books*, October 21, 2004, and at TomDispatch.com, November 5, 2004.

© 2008 New Left Review. "Afghanistan: Mirage of the Good War" by Tariq Ali. First published by *New Left Review*, March–April 2008.

© 2009 *Le Monde diplomatique*, English edition. "Afghanistan: Chaos Central" by Chris Sands. First published by *Le Monde diplomatique*'s English edition, February 2009.

© 2009 Ann Jones. "Meet the Afghan Army: Is It a Figment of Washington's Imagination?" by Ann Jones. First published at TomDispatch.com, September 20, 2009.

© 2009 Pratap Chatterjee. "Paying Off the Warlords: Anatomy of an Afghan Culture of Corruption" by Pratap Chatterjee. First published at TomDispatch.com, November 17, 2009.

© 2009 The Nation. "How the US Funds the Taliban" by Aram Roston. First published by *The Nation*, November 30, 2009.

© 2009 The Nation. "Remember the Women?" by Ann Jones. First published by *The Nation*, November 9, 2009.

© 2009 Elsa Rassbach. "The US Government Has Never Supported Democratic Organizations." Elsa Rassbach interviews Zoya of the Foreign Committee of RAWA. First published at ZNet, May 23, 2009.

© 2009 Tom Engelhardt. "Going for Broke: Six Ways the Af-Pak War Is Expanding" by Tom Engelhardt. First published at TomDispatch.com, May 21, 2009.

© 2010 Tom Engelhardt and Nick Turse. "The Shadow War: Making Sense of the New CIA Battlefield in Afghanistan" by Tom Engelhardt and Nick Turse. First published at TomDispatch.com, January 10, 2010.

© 2010 Nick Turse. "The 700 Military Bases of Afghanistan: Black Sites in the Empire of Bases" by Nick Turse. First published at TomDispatch.com, February 9, 2010.

© 2009 Middle East Institute. "How Hearts and Minds Were Lost in

ABOUT THE AUTHORS

Tariq Ali is a writer and filmmaker. He has written more than two dozen books on world history and politics, and seven novels (translated into over a dozen languages) as well as scripts for the stage and screen. He is an editor of *New Left Review* and lives in London.

Andrew J. Bacevich, professor of history and international relations at Boston University, retired from the US Army with the rank of colonel. His latest book is *Washington Rules: America's Path to Permanent War*.

Dominique Bari is a correspondent for *L'Humanité* ("Humanity"). Its English-language website is www.humaniteinenglish.com.

Sir Rodric Braithwaite was British ambassador to Moscow, 1988–92. His book *Afgantsy: The Russians in Afghanistan 1979–1989* is to be published by Profile Books in March 2011.

Pratap Chatterjee is a freelance journalist and senior editor at CorpWatch who has traveled extensively in Afghanistan and Iraq. He has written two books about the war on terror, *Iraq, Inc.* (Seven Stories Press, 2004) and *Halliburton's Army* (Nation Books, 2009).

Juan R. I. Cole is Richard P. Mitchell Collegiate Professor of History at the University of Michigan. For three decades, he has sought to put the relationship of the West and the Muslim world in historical context. His most recent book is *Engaging the Muslim World* (Palgrave Macmillan, 2009). He has written, edited, or translated fifteen books, and authored sixty-five journal articles and chapters. He is the proprietor of the Informed Comment weblog on current affairs.

Robert D. Crews is Associate Professor of History at Stanford University and co-editor, with Amin Tarzi, of *The Taliban and the Crisis of Afghanistan* (Harvard University Press).

Robert Dreyfuss, a *Nation* contributing editor, is an investigative journalist in Alexandria, Virginia, specializing in politics and national security. He is the author of *Devil's Game: How the United States Helped Unleash Fundamentalist Islam* and is a frequent contributor to *Rolling Stone, The American Prospect,* and *Mother Jones.*

Tom Engelhardt, co-founder of the *American Empire Project,* runs the Nation Institute's TomDispatch.com. He is the author of *The End of Victory Culture,* a history of the Cold War and beyond, as well as of a novel, *The Last Days of Publishing.* His latest book, *The American Way of War* (Haymarket Books), was published in May 2010.

Zabih Farhad (pseudonym) worked as an interpreter for US and ISAF forces in Afghanistan for five years.

Graham E. Fuller is a former CIA station chief in Kabul and a former vice-chair of the CIA's National Intelligence Council. He is author of numerous books on the Middle East, including *The Future of Political Islam.*

Chalmers Johnson is the author of *Blowback* (2000), *The Sorrows of Empire* (2004), *Nemesis: The Last Days of the American Republic* (2006), and *Dismantling the Empire* (2010). From 1967 to 1973, Johnson served as a consultant to the CIA's Office of National Estimates.

Ann Jones, author of *Kabul in Winter,* does humanitarian work in postconflict zones with NGOs and the United Nations.

Malalai Joya has been called "the bravest woman in Afghanistan." At a constitutional assembly in Kabul in 2003, she stood up and denounced her country's powerful NATO-backed warlords. She was twenty-five years old. Two years later, she became the youngest person elected to Afghanistan's new Parliament. In 2007, she was suspended from Parliament for her persistent criticism of the warlords and drug barons and their cronies. She has survived four assassination attempts to date, is accompanied at all times by armed guards, and sleeps only in safe houses. Her memoir was published in the United States as *A Woman Among Warlords* and in the United Kingdom as *Raising My Voice*.

Oleg Vasilevich Kustov served in the Soviet and Russian armed forces for thirty-seven years, including twenty-seven in military intelligence.

Elsa Rassbach is a filmmaker and writer. She is a US citizen who presently lives in Berlin, where she is active in the German and European peace and justice movements.

Aram Roston is an investigative journalist and the author of *The Man Who Pushed America to War: The Extraordinary Life, Adventures, and Obsessions of Ahmad Chalabi* (Nation Books, 2008).

Chris Sands is Afghanistan correspondent for *The National* in Abu Dhabi and a co-founder of Makoto Photographic Agency. He has lived in Kabul since 2005.

ABOUT NICK TURSE

Nick Turse is an award-winning journalist, historian, essayist, and the associate editor of the Nation Institute's TomDispatch.com. He is the author of *The Complex: How the Military Invades Our Everyday Lives* (Metropolitan Books/Henry Holt, 2008) and has written for *The Los Angeles Times*, *The San Francisco Chronicle*, *The Nation*, GOOD magazine, *Le Monde diplomatique* (English- and German- language), *In These Times*, and *The Village Voice*, among other print and online publications. His articles have also appeared in such newspapers as *The Atlanta Journal-Constitution*, *The Baltimore Sun*, *The Chicago Tribune*, and *The Seattle Times*, among others.

Turse was the recipient of a Ridenhour Prize at the National Press Club in April 2009 for his years-long investigation of mass civilian slaughter by US troops in Vietnam's Mekong Delta in 1968–1969. In his article for *The Nation* "A My Lai a Month," he also exposed a Pentagon-level cover-up of these crimes that was abetted by a major news magazine. In 2009 he also received a James Aronson Award for the same article.

Turse edited this volume while a fellow at New York University's Center for the United States and the Cold War. He is currently at work on *Kill Anything That Moves*, a history of US atrocities during the Vietnam War, for Metropolitan Books/Henry Holt. He was awarded a Guggenheim Fellowship for work on *Kill Anything That Moves*.